the
transformative
power of

A rebuilt Book

SMALL
GROUPS

"Our small-group friends at Church of the Nativity help us to see Jesus in our everyday lives. Recently, we shared a heartache with our group, and in that vulnerable moment, they listened and leaned in close. They prayed with us, and we bonded in our brokenness. We felt safe, secure, and loved. Our fellow small-group members were Jesus with skin on."

Beth and Dan Morrison
Church of the Nativity
Timonium, Maryland

"Like many parishes, St. Hilary began as a parish with a few small groups, such as the men's group and the women's group. Following the small-group model developed by Fr. Michael White and Tom Corcoran, we transformed our parish into a parish of small groups. In a matter of months, the number of small groups at St. Hilary doubled, and half the people who attend Mass each weekend were in small groups. I am hearing stories of friendships formed and lives changed. I recommend *The Transformative Power of Small Groups* for anyone looking to revive their parish and build a structure for growth and deepening of faith."

Fr. Roger G. Gustafson
Pastor, St. Hilary Church and School
Tiburon, California

"Faith sharing in small groups is the 'secret sauce' to building community and igniting discipleship in any parish. *The Transformative Power of Small Groups* is essential reading for any parish that wants to form disciples who are on fire with the Holy Spirit. Fr. Michael White and Tom Corcoran speak firsthand from their proven experience of building a healthy and growing small-group ministry in their parish. Read this book and discover the vibrant, effective path they cultivated."

Most Rev. Adam J. Parker
Auxiliary Bishop of Baltimore

the
transformative
power of

A rebuilt Book

SMALL
GROUPS

*A 7-Step Guide for Building
Vibrant Catholic Communities*

Michael White and Tom Corcoran

Ave Maria Press AVE Notre Dame, Indiana

Nihil Obstat: Reverend Monsignor Michael Heintz, PhD
                   Censor Librorum

Imprimatur: Most Reverend Kevin C. Rhoades
                   Bishop of Fort Wayne–South Bend
                   Given at Fort Wayne, Indiana, on September 17, 2024

Founded in 1865, Ave Maria Press is a ministry of the United States Province of Holy Cross.

www.avemariapress.com

Paperback: ISBN-13 978-1-64680-346-0

E-book: ISBN-13 978-1-64680-347-7

Cover and text design by Andy Wagoner.

Printed and bound in the United States of America.

Library of Congress Cataloging-in-Publication Data is available.

| Contents |

Step VI: Serve Your Groups

Step VII: Persevere

Appendixes

| Introduction |

When we wrote *Rebuilt: Awakening the Faithful, Reaching the Lost, Making Church Matter* (2013, Ave Maria Press), we sought to cover a wide spectrum of parish life and ministry based on lessons learned and insights gained from our combined pastoral experience at Church of the Nativity in suburban Baltimore. Since that time, we have enjoyed getting to know and work with parishes and parish staff from every part of the United States and several other countries as well. Perhaps the number one area of interest about which we receive questions is our parish-based faith-sharing communities that we call small groups. How do parishes get them started? How do they keep them going? And most critically, how do they motivate parishioners to make the commitment and investment in small groups? This was information we were eager to share because our small-group experience has been a game changer in the ongoing renewal of our parish.

It is true that we started our small-group journey with absolutely no conception of what groups are supposed to be or *why* we should have them. We just saw them consistently as part of church life in most of the successful (admittedly mostly evangelical) communities we studied as we sought to renew our parish. If they promoted small groups as a vital exercise in building healthy, vibrant churches of fully engaged Christ followers, and if they considered small groups as *the* key to increased participation, that was good enough for us. We didn't get it, but we went with it.

Our journey began by mimicking others (actually, it was more like slavishly aping successful churches). But over the last twenty years, we have personally seen the purpose and the power of small groups in our parish. Their ability to provide pastoral care to parishioners, far beyond what we could do ourselves, deeply impressed us. We have seen the effectiveness of small groups building fellowship and strengthening unity among our members. Countless lifelong friendships and hardwired connections in Christ have resulted from small-group ministry in our parish. Most significantly, small groups have been vital in creating a discipleship culture where people don't just sit in the pews and "consume" but take personal responsibility for developing a Christlike character. We should also add that the two of us have grown in our faith as a result of our small-group experiences.

We wrote this book to help get you started on your small-group journey or assist you in taking small groups to a whole new level at your parish. If new to small groups, you will soon discover that theories and thoughts abound on how to launch, promote, maintain, and grow a successful small-group ministry. While we will offer some basic theory on the topic, this book really is about motivating you and moving you to take action in bringing small-group life to more and more people in your parish.

We will share with you what has worked for us (and what hasn't) in starting a small-group ministry from scratch. When we began serving at the parish, as already noted, we didn't even know small-group ministry existed, much less how to build one. As we write this book, we have gone from literally no one in small groups and a parish culture suspicious of the very idea to nearly 2,500 active small-group members today. Admittedly, we are a big parish, so that's a big number, but more important, it is an impressive percentage of our total population, representing about 45 percent of registered adult parishioners.

As we mentioned, the available information and resources on small-group ministry abound, and we will be citing some of them. We freely confess that there are practitioners of small groups with far greater experience and wisdom than we have. We don't know everything about running a small-group ministry. No one does. But we want to share with you what we do know. Our goals for this book are simple, and they are threefold.

Our *first goal* is to simply share with you lessons we have learned in our parish. We want to take what is in our "cup," in terms of experience and insight, and pour it into your cup. We will share with you what has worked here at Nativity that you can adopt and apply to your setting. The book is filled with transferrable principles, but it will require your leadership to transfer them. You'll have to figure out the cultural fit of small groups in your community. It calls for leadership to cast a vision and work out the details of that vision in your specific context.

Our *second goal* is to help you get excited about the impact small groups will have in your parish. As you read about our experience and the stories of lives changed, it will give you the fuel you need to undertake the rewarding, yet challenging, work of launching and building a small-group ministry.

Our *third goal* is to offer a step-by-step process for launching small groups at your parish. We want to shape the path for you to get started and keep going. To that end, we lay out the book in seven steps you can take on your small-group journey. While we talk about "steps," we really don't live our lives in a linear fashion. Most of our experience is not like assembling IKEA furniture, in which we finish step 1 and, once done with it, move on to step 2. In real life, we usually go back and forth between steps. Or we take a step forward and then realize we missed something important and have to backtrack. And some steps just have to be taken over and over again.

Despite the limitation of laying the book out in steps, we think they'll get you moving. While reading about groups can be helpful, we have found that the best way to really learn about what works when it comes to small-group life is to start moving. As two Jesuit-trained alumni, we are very much fans of St. Ignatius Loyola's encouragement to be "contemplatives in action." Move, take action, reflect upon it, and then move again.

Here are the seven steps:

Step I: Know the *Why*

In the first step, we want to ground you in a vision for building a small-group ministry. Our experience notwithstanding, it is better to know why you are doing groups rather than just copying another parish.

Step II: Recognize the Benefits

Building a small-group program takes effort, especially in the beginning. You will probably experience some fits and starts as well as frustrations. But it's essential to know that it is all worth it. In this step, we want to give you language to help you get members of your parish on board, as well as the motivation you will need to keep going.

Step III: Build Your Team

This step is crucial, so as you will see, we spend a great deal of time on it. This is the step most quickly and easily overlooked, and yet the most vital to building a sustainable and successful small-group ministry. We will lay out for you a framework for building your team and explain the roles and responsibilities for your team members.

Step IV: Define the *What*

Often this step is daunting for small-group leaders. Groups need *content* so that conversations will be well directed and stay focused on the purpose of discipleship. Successful small-group ministries need a *content plan* as well as established and shared *values* to be adhered to by each group. Determining the content and values of groups keeps members unified, connected to the parish, and focused on the message of the Gospel and the purpose of discipleship.

Step V: Launch Your Groups

At some point, it will be time to launch or expand groups in the parish. In this section, we will help you decide when to start and whether to start small or go big. And we will be showing our hand on what we think you should do.

Step VI: Serve Your Groups

In this section, we will look at some of the day-to-day responsibilities of running a small group. This step will help you find answers to your practical questions that arise from leading small-group ministry.

Step VII: Persevere

Building any successful ministry means long obedience in the same direction. Here we'll discuss developing an *annual plan* for small groups to help you do that. We will end with encouragement aimed at motivating you to keep going and moving.

So, that's it. Those are the steps. We are glad you are on this small-group journey with us. As the oft-cited proverb goes, a journey of a thousand miles begins with just a single step. Let's take that first step.

STEP I
Know the *Why*

| 1 |

Knowing the *Why* behind the *What*

People don't buy what you do, they buy why you do it.

—Simon Sinek

When you lose your *why*, you lose your *way*. On the other hand, when you *discover* your why, you *find* your way. So, while our small-group story started by simply copying others (as we described in the introduction), this chapter is offered to ground you in the reason for undertaking small groups in the first place.

Our why comes from Jesus's final instruction to his disciples. Before ascending into heaven, Jesus told the eleven remaining apostles, "All power in heaven and on earth has been given to me. Go, therefore, and make disciples of all nations" (Mt 28:18–19).

Jesus leaves his friends and followers a mission so simple no one could be unclear about it and a vision so big every generation since has been working on it. The Church exists to make disciples. We are here to lead people into a growing relationship with Jesus Christ. That's our mission. And we exist to make disciples of *all* nations. That's the vision. And yet, despite Jesus's clarity, we churchpeople often lose sight of that mission and vision. As a consequence, it is essential to come back to it over and over again.

In serving the mission and pursuing the vision Jesus gave us, we have discovered that successful growing parishes have *four* foundational principles that help them stay focused and keep going.

1. Successful parishes build layers of leaders.

These parishes understand that everything rises and falls on leadership—and not just one stand-out star or celebrity pastor. Instead, they develop leaders at every level of parish life: clergy and parish staff, as well as volunteer leaders. In a subsequent chapter you will see how important it is to build layers of leaders when it comes to small-group ministry and how to do it.

2. Healthy, growing parishes create an *excellent weekend* experience.

By this we mean the weekend liturgies and the programs and ministries that surround them. The Mass is the source and summit of parish life, feeding parishioners on the Eucharistic Lord. But it is the entire weekend experience that sets the tone and builds the culture of a parish. When done well it can be a powerful catalyst for people to grow in faith. Later, we will discuss how to leverage the weekend experience to encourage people into small groups.

3. Parishes grow wider by *welcoming outsiders*.

Jesus came to seek and save the lost, so growing, healthy parishes care about people disconnected from Christ and his Church. As others have noted, the parish is most attractive when our charity is most convincing. When small groups are working well in a parish they lead to a more loving community, making the community more appealing.

4. Successful, growing parishes help people go deeper.

This is done by shaping a *clear discipleship path*. They identify the habits that help people grow in understanding and practicing their faith. Our book *Rebuilt Faith* details and offers reflections on the *steps of discipleship* we have found absolutely essential to rebuilding a healthy parish community. One of those steps is engaging in Christian community through small groups. For people in your parish to grow as committed Christ followers, a small group can be a powerful experience. But we have found that small groups often help people also grow in every other area of discipleship—they give more, they pray more, they serve more, they more often share their faith!

While small groups are vital, it is important to understand *why* they are vital, namely, the role they play in helping people grow in their faith. Sometimes parish leaders put the wrong emphasis on small groups, perhaps seeing them as a place for adult education or Bible study. There's nothing wrong with faith formation programs; they're just not the point of small groups. The point and the power of groups comes in relationships. It begins with God himself. God is a God of relationships; it is within the nature of God to be relational. God is not alone, God is a community of Father, Son, and Spirit. Each person of the Trinity is in relationship with another.

Out of that community of Divine Persons, we see that God builds a relationship with his children. We do not simply relate to God as Creator; rather, we are invited to call God Father and live in an intimate relationship with him. As Paul writes in Romans, "For you did not receive a spirit of slavery to fall back into fear, but you received a spirit of adoption, through which we cry, 'Abba, Father!' The Spirit itself bears witness with our spirit that we are children of God" (Rom 8:15–16).

Out of the community of the Trinity we can also know the Son as a brother and a friend. Jesus tells the apostles in the Gospel of John, "I have called you friends, because I have told you everything I have heard from my Father" (Jn 15:15). The apostles start out as strangers who don't really know Jesus or, in some cases, one another. But over time they become his closest friends and followers. Jesus didn't just call the apostles to undertake the work of the Church, he wanted to enjoy a deep relationship with them in which he could call them friends.

We see Jesus emphasize relationships throughout his teaching. When he was asked about the greatest commandment, he cited not just one but rather *two* commands. He said, "You shall love the Lord, your God, with all your heart, with all your soul, and with all your mind. This is the greatest and the first commandment. The second is like it: You shall love your neighbor as yourself. The whole law and the prophets depend on these two commandments" (Mt 22:37–40). Jesus taught that a healthy respect for and relationship with God leads to a healthy relationship with others.

Finally, out of the community of the Trinity, we see the relational nature of God in the Holy Spirit. It was the Spirit who anointed the early church, the church of the apostles, moving it most purposefully and most powerfully. And it is in the Spirit that Christ's followers easily connected relationally as a community. For example, Acts of the Apostles says: "Every day they devoted themselves to meeting together in the temple area and to breaking bread in their homes. They ate their meals with exultation and sincerity of heart" (Acts 2:46).

The emphasis on relationship and fellowship continues in the work of St. Paul. Much of Paul's teaching and preaching provides advice and instruction to the early church about how to live in community. For example, in both his letters to the Corinthians, he forthrightly addresses their internal conflicts and how to resolve divisions so they can live well together as a church family and grow as disciples. In fact, this is a pronounced theme throughout the corpus of Paul's epistles to the various churches. For example:

Be devoted and honor one another. Romans 12:10

Love one another. Romans 13:8

Accept one another. Romans 15:7

Greet one another. 1 Corinthians 16:20

Serve one another. Galatians 5:13

Be kind and compassionate to one another. Ephesians 4:32

Forgive one another. Ephesians 4:32

And that is only naming a few, hardly an exhaustive list. Other New Testament letters bring additional relational advice: we are reminded to encourage one another and pray for each other in James 5:16, and offer hospitality to one another in 1 Peter 4:9.

Think about it: these are apostolic exhortations to the Church that can be lived out only in a faith community where we can be known, loved, and cared for, and where we can know, love, and care for other Christ followers.

Others have written important reflections on the relational nature of God and the importance of Christian community. Our point here is that small groups can play a vital role in the life of your parish in reflecting the relational and communal nature of God and the message of the New Testament. Building a small-group ministry acknowledges the value God places on relationships and understands that without community, without friends in faith, we cannot grow into fully devoted followers of Jesus Christ.

As the two of us write about the importance of community in our faith development, we recognize the deep irony that *we* are making this acknowledgment, because this is not our natural bent. For a long time, we both saw faith as a completely solitary exercise. Like many Catholics, we thought our faith was both personal and private. Our particular personality type fights against the communal nature of faith: we both have strong, introverted tendencies and enjoy alone time as *the* way in which we renew and recharge. We both prefer task-driven activities to relational ones. Neither one of us loves parties.

So, if some part of you pushes back against groups and feels they are intrusive into your personal space, an infringement on your privacy, we absolutely understand. However, as we have led our parish, we have learned to lean into the importance and the power of relationships when it comes to our faith. Like us, as you reflect on your faith journey, you may recognize the power of others in your formation as a follower of Christ. Without certain providential relationships, you would have never come to know Jesus as Lord or come to follow him in any serious way. When Peter makes his confession of faith at Caesarea Philippi (Mt 16:16), Jesus reveals to him that he is blessed because he didn't come to this insight on his own. He had some help from both God the Father, who imparted it to him at that critical moment, and Jesus himself, who led him to it step-by-step. For most of us, that help comes through the faith inspired by the example of other Christ followers.

> **Tom:** For me, the early example of my parents, Mary Ann and Don, and my maternal grandfather, Thomas, led me to understand Christianity. I saw them live out their faith in a transparent and compellingly authentic way. But my faith grew to a new level when I started dating my college girlfriend (now wife) Mia. For the first time, I had a friend who loved God and wanted to follow him

as a dedicated disciple. I had someone I could discuss my faith, share my struggles, and grow with. Since then, other friends in faith have continued to fuel my faith through the years by participating in small groups in our parish. I have been inspired by the faith of friends like Ron, Steve, Brian, Mark, and Chris, to name a few. Those names mean nothing to you, but to me they are companions on my journey as a disciple of Jesus Christ.

God is a God of relationships. God is a God of community. Building a small-group ministry is all about creating an environment where the people in our pews can experience a community that reflects the beauty and truth of the Trinity. It is about leveraging relationships so that people grow as fully devoted followers of Christ. Small groups build relationships that lead people to experience genuine Christian community. This is the *why* behind the *what*.

FOR REFLECTION AND CONVERSATION

1. Of the scripture passages mentioned in this chapter, which one resonates most deeply with you?

2. Which people have been vital in helping you come to faith and grow as a Christ follower? Take some time to write down their names, prayerfully remembering each of them.

3. Where do you see small groups in your parish's overall strategy of making disciples?

| 2 |

Committing to One Key Decision

Decision making is the specific executive task.

—Peter Drucker

For small groups to succeed and flourish, you must make one key decision. And it may seem like a very small matter on the surface. The first time we heard about this, we didn't get it. However, after just a few years into our small-group journey, we came to see this decision as absolutely critical and crucial to the success of our small-group ministry. And it will be absolutely critical and crucial to the success of your small-group ministry and the health of your parish too. So, don't sweat it much: only the whole direction of your parish weighs in the balance. (Okay, maybe we are exaggerating a little, but *just* a little.)

Here is the decision you need to make: Do you want to be a church *of* small groups or a church *with* small groups? You may be thinking, "I want to be right. Which is the right choice? I want that one." Or maybe you are thinking, "What's the difference? You seem to be making a big deal out of two prepositions." As we mentioned, we didn't get it either when we first heard it, so allow us to make sense of the distinction.

11

A church *with* small groups means that groups are something you do along with other things, such as Friday night bingo. You offer small groups as one among many programs. Every once in a while, you promote this program to parishioners, maybe running an ad in the bulletin. You give it to a volunteer to organize on whatever spare money you can squeeze out of your budget, or perhaps you provide no budget at all. From time to time, you check in on them. When someone mentions small groups, you can say, "Yeah, we do that in our parish." It's a perfectly fine choice. We won't judge you for it, we made the same choice getting started.

But you will need to set expectations for group life. In other words, make sure everyone understands the desired outcomes. Your small-group program will always be of limited appeal because of your limited investment. As a consequence, your group program will have a limited impact on the life of the parish. And you will not experience all the benefits of small groups that we discuss in the next two chapters.

Father Michael: If you are an advocate in your parish for small groups and your pastor or the parish leadership doesn't fully support the idea, we do not want the preceding paragraph to demoralize you. But if the parish leadership has given you the green light, or even a yellow light, to start small groups in only a modest way, run with it. Because as you get people into groups and they have a good experience, you may be able to convince the pastor and parish leadership to make more of a commitment to groups. And even if you never influence leadership to make groups a priority, it is worth your energy and effort to invest in the people who *will* get into the small groups you are able to start.

Of course, as you have guessed by now, we advocate choosing to be a parish *of* small groups. This means that you make small groups core to your parish's ministry, a decision stemming from a desire for every single member of your parish to be growing as disciples.

Here are the practical ways to build a church of small groups:

1. Preach and communicate the value of groups (over and over . . . and over again).

Communicate something sixty-four thousand times if you want to get people to buy into a new idea. This might be a slight exaggeration, but something important bears repeating if you want to give it traction. Communicating the value of groups means we look for opportunities to discuss them. This is especially important in the first few years of launching a small-group ministry.

Communicating the value of groups can mean anything from a whole homily on the topic one weekend to a homily series over the course of several weekends (we'll be explaining homily series subsequently). It might mean special announcements at Mass, a bulletin insert, lobby posters. It might mean all of the above.

When you decide to be a church *of* small groups, you are deciding that you will promote small groups through all avenues of communication at your disposal. In addition, you commit to *consistent communication* so that every member of your church knows you offer groups and that you want them to get involved in group life. Here's one clue about groups: when you think you have said too much about them, that is probably when members of the parish are really hearing about them for the first time.

2. Celebrate small-group launches.

We will dive into greater detail later in the book about *how* to run a small-group launch weekend in your parish. Here, it is important to know that to have a church of small groups, you will need to set aside one or even two weekends of the year when you invite all the members of your parish to join a small group. We have found the best times to launch groups are in September at the beginning of the school year, in January with the start of a new year, and before the season of Lent when people are looking to do a little something extra for their faith.

3. Eliminate competing systems.

Okay, this is where the rubber hits the road. This is where we might offend you (if we haven't already). This is where we might be setting you up to experience some conflict. This is where you have to make some tough decisions and deal with difficult circumstances. As the saying goes, reality is a tough place to live, but it's the only place where you can get a good steak.

Here's the reality: the people in your parish have only so much free time, and church time is carved out of their free time. At parishes, we often have so many events going on and activities running that we don't stop to consider what we really want people to do. We are often *unintentional* about what we invite parishioners to participate in.

At Church of the Nativity, we are clear that when it comes to your church time, if you are going to give more than an hour a week at Mass, we want your next investment of time to be in a small group. We can make this crystal clear because we have eliminated the systems competing with small-group ministry at our parish. Eliminating competing systems means getting rid of, or being disciplined enough to begin to remove, what we refer to as "pseudo-fellowship." Pseudo-fellowship is when people gather at the parish for some purpose other than the steps of discipleship, and it usually takes one of two forms.

One is fundraisers: spaghetti dinners, golf tournaments, spring carnivals, fall festivals. Many times, people defend fundraisers not only because they make money but also because the shared effort creates community. Yet, they rarely build enduring bonds among parishioners, as the rate of burnout for many parish volunteers sadly attests. Meanwhile, fundraisers often weaken what we see as an essential understanding of the connection between faith and finances (as we explain in our book *ChurchMoney*).

The second style of pseudo-fellowship usually takes the form of fundraisers dressed up as entertainment or social gatherings, for instance, seasonal concerts, holiday parties, dinner theater. While these events can be fun (so they might very well have their place), they aren't drawing people's hearts and lives into discipleship. And in fact, such pseudo-fellowship is also fast disappearing from parish life entirely as more and more parishioners look less and less to their parish for leisure-time activities.

We acknowledge that some parishes do have really wonderful, inclusive, discipleship-affirming social events that by all means should be maintained. But often the opposite is true, and when we as church leaders invest time, energy, and parish resources in these events, we water down and weaken the message that small groups are the place for community. So, as you begin your small-group journey, commit to eliminating those activities from the life of the parish. Be ruthless, but be smart. Don't dramatically or impulsively cancel long-standing and often-beloved programs. You could start a war. Instead, begin taking the focus off those programs and, instead, start announcing, promoting, and celebrating small groups.

We also acknowledge the reality of parish life and know that you might not be able to bring that kind of focus and discipline to your small-group effort all at once or even over the course of several seasons. You may need to have conversations with volunteers in the parish. On the other hand, some of the people who lead these events and fundraisers might be ready to let them go.

> **Father Michael:** We used to host an event called "Breakfast with Santa" each Advent. Along with Santa, we offered crafts and games and other activities. But of course, breakfast was a pretty important part. It was a big production because it required the effort of dozens of volunteers and pretty much two days of concentrated work in the middle of the busy holiday season.
>
> Eventually, we realized there were better ways to raise disciples (not to mention money) than flipping pancakes. Seeing the impact and life changes happening in our small-group program made it obvious to us that we had outgrown Santa. Even though we knew we were right, still, we made the announcement to the event team with trepidation. We need not have. The team leader, Charlie, eventually met with me, with tears in his eyes, to thank us on behalf of his whole crew for giving them back the weekend before Christmas.

One way to move people beyond pseudo-fellowship is to model small-group fellowship for them, giving them an experience of it. We work to replicate small-group life in meetings and other gatherings parishioners are already attending. For example, when we bring our parents together for sacramental preparation for their children's Baptism, First Reconciliation, and First Communion, we set aside time in the program for small-group "table" discussion. This lets parents connect in a circle and talk about what it feels like to be a first-time parent or the basic challenges of raising kids.

In our Order of Christian Initiation of Adults (OCIA) program, we also create a small-group atmosphere with plenty of opportunities for small-group sharing. When the formal period of mystagogy is complete, we invite them to continue to meet as a small group or find a new one.

Recently, we started dads' small groups that meet on Sundays while their kids are in their faith formation class—which also has a small-group format. Previously, the dads just sat around drinking coffee and texting while waiting for their kids. The dads' small groups are meant to expose them to the benefits of small-group life with minimal commitment.

True Christian fellowship means we are helping one another become fully devoted followers of Christ. We are praying with one another, talking to each other, sharing our joys, and bearing one another's burdens. You can build a church of small groups if you are willing to commit to this one key decision and work to focus the parish on this new direction.

FOR REFLECTION AND CONVERSATION

1. What does it mean to you to be a church *of* small groups? Is this a commitment you can make?

2. Name the ways you can start to talk about small groups in your parish.

3. Are there competing systems to small groups that you need to eliminate? Make a list. On a scale of 1 to 5, how difficult will it be to eliminate them? What are one or two ways you can add small-group experiences to what you are already doing?

STEP II

Recognize the Benefits

| 3 |

Recognizing the Benefits of Small-Group Life

We have all known the long loneliness
and we have learned that the only solution is love
and that love comes with community.

—Dorothy Day

As a reader of this book, you're either considering the value of launching a small-group program at your parish or working to convince others, perhaps your pastor, that groups are worth the effort. Or maybe you just want to give the group experience a try with a small circle of friends. In this chapter, you will find reliable benefits that a small group almost always provides. By building a small-group ministry, parishioners and parish staff will experience these benefits in their lives and come to grow stronger in their faith. So, if someone asks what the benefits of small groups are or why the parish should offer them, you can say, "I'm glad you asked."

1. Small groups help us find friends in faith.

Our friends influence the quality and direction of our lives. Peer pressure is not just a middle school phenomenon. As human beings, we are influenced by the people with whom we spend time. Don't believe us? Just notice how you start using the same words and phrases or facial expressions and gestures as other people around you use. Reflect for a moment on the many times you make a decision based on how other people will think or react. In fact, time after time, study after study shows that our financial status and physical well-being are dramatically affected by the people who surround us. While we don't technically need friendship for survival, it does add value to our living and joy to our lives. And since our friends *will* determine the direction, and sometimes even the quality, of our lives, we can either have it work *for* us or *against* us when it comes to our faith life. Without friends *in faith*, we have to manage our relationships and resist peer pressure to grow as followers of Christ all alone and on our own. With friends in faith, our relationships work for us. Proverbs says it this way: "Walk with the wise and you become wise, but the companion of fools fares badly" (Prv 13:20).

In small groups, we meet companions on our spiritual journey who can grow to become our friends because groups are a *pathway* to friendship. As St. Paul writes, "With such affection for you, we were determined to share with you not only the gospel of God, but our very selves as well, so dearly beloved had you become to us" (1 Thes 2:8).

Some people push back on groups and say, "I don't need any more friends. I have enough friends." Are you sure? Our experience is that most people do not have many friends, much less *any* friends in faith. We all have friends in our life who are friends of convenience, friends formed by mere proximity or affinity, and friendships that are the fruit of shared seasons of life. But rare is the friendship born of faith unless we put ourselves in an environment where we can form such friendships. Something powerful happens when we find that people whose company we enjoy are also people who can help us grow in our relationship with Christ. Small groups create special bonds of friendship.

Tom: One example for me is my friend Chris, who joined my small group fifteen years ago. Over the intervening years, we've grown to become great friends, such good friends, in fact, that I asked Chris to serve as godfather to my son Kepha. In all that time, we've discovered many shared interests and undertaken a number of projects together. It's a friendship that has brought real value to my life and the life of my family. But it's a friendship that would not have happened without group life.

2. Groups are a place to mutually encourage one another in faith.

In his Letter to the Romans, Paul writes, "For I long to see you, that I may share with you some spiritual gift so that you may be strengthened, that is, that you and I may be mutually encouraged by one another's faith, yours and mine" (Rom 1:11–12).

Paul looked forward to visiting the Church in Rome so he could learn from them and be encouraged by them. Think about that. Consider Paul and his story. He was a spiritual giant. Knowing the Hebrew Scriptures from beginning to end, he also had a complete command of classical philosophy, enabling him to argue with the greatest Jewish scholars and Greek philosophers of the day. He was a linguist and moved comfortably in different cultures. Writing roughly half of the New Testament, he established church communities all over the Roman Empire. He willingly suffered stoning, beating, and a shipwreck so that others would know the Lord. He had a personal encounter with the risen Jesus.

Yet, as epic as Paul's journey had been, as staggeringly accomplished as he was, and as towering as his faith stood, he told the Romans he *needed* to learn from their faith. He needed their faith to encourage and strengthen him. And if Paul needed to be encouraged by others' faith, then we do too. Groups provide an environment where you can learn from other people's faith. No matter how mature you are, or think you are, regardless of how long you've been a practicing Catholic or active in your parish, you have something to *learn* from others. Likewise, no matter how fresh your faith or how tentative your prayers, you have something to *share* with others. If you are new to church, for instance, your interest and enthusiasm can be incredibly encouraging to people who have forgotten that stage of faith. Each of us can learn and be learned from. It's as simple as that.

One of the amazing and surprising perks of small-group life is seeing people connect who would not have known each other outside a group environment. People of diverse backgrounds and interests, perhaps coming from different communities, who would probably never encounter each other in social settings often get to know each other in groups, enriching one another in the process.

> **Tom:** One of my favorite examples of this is my friend Steve. Steve has an encyclopedic knowledge of the Bible and loves God's Word deeply. But he resisted getting into a small group, being a bit of an introvert for whom faith is personal and private. Several years ago, after challenging him on this for an extended period of time, he agreed to give a group a try. To his surprise, he ended up in a small group with younger guys who, having been raised Catholic, were less grounded in scripture. Deftly but effectively, he awakened in his group an interest and enthusiasm for the Word of God, equipping them to be much more confident

in their faith. In the process, Steve found his own commitment to scripture refreshed and renewed.

3. Groups lead to positive life change and growth.

Conversion and life change are all part of Christian living. We are not yet who God has created us to be. We have faults and failures we need to walk away from and leave behind. Each of us has rough edges to our character that must be chiseled away and polished over. We have thought patterns that should be corrected. Small groups provide an environment where we can learn, if only slowly, new patterns of thinking and form better habits for living. The more we have conversations about following Christ—with others who follow Christ—the more easily we become like him. As Proverbs says, "Iron is sharpened by iron; one person sharpens another" (Prv 27:17).

God made us to learn from other people's experiences and examples. When people sit in a circle and share their stories, they can grow in an understanding of how life works, and when they share their story of faith, they can grow in an understanding of how faith works. It is no mere coincidence that conversation and conversion have the same roots in Latin. Throughout our lives, our conversations change us. And sometimes they move us; they convert us. The power of small groups comes from forming relationships in which *conversations* lead to *conversion*.

> **Father Michael:** A few years ago, we asked members to share with us their positive experiences with small groups. One parishioner, Bob, wrote this: "Though resistant at first, it's been powerful for my wife and me to meet with other couples and share our faith, as well as challenges in our faith.

But our small group has actually helped us to connect as a couple in our faith for the first time since we've been married. Now we are not just learning to share faith with our group; we're getting better at sharing our faith with each other."

4. Small groups are relationships that support our *other* relationships.

We get into groups so that other Christ followers can help us apply the "Golden Rule," a maxim of reciprocity found in nearly every major world religion from ancient times. It simply teaches to "do unto others what you would have them do to you." The Golden Rule is basic to Christian living and is completely countercultural. That is because it represents the way of God's kingdom and *not* the way of the world. We need voices speaking into our lives, reminding us about kingdom values when we inevitably encounter problems in our daily experiences. A safe place where we can process those conflicts in a Christian context is essential for health and wholeness.

Think about it: with your work associates, among your classmates, and even at home in your family relationships, you have to be *on*. People want and need something *from* you; they have expectations for you, who and what they think you should be. In most every environment you find yourself in and in whatever role you hold, you need to maintain a certain level of professionalism, if not pretense. The ties you form are intended to serve the business of your organization. At home, there is most definitely a certain performance, as a parent, spouse, or sibling, that is expected of you. Those relationships can be challenging. We need support in managing them in a positive way.

Small groups are a place where, other than being *honest* and honestly transparent about who you really are, there are no expectations *on you* or about *you*. You can safely bring your struggles and challenges with others to the group because these are people who have no vested interest in the situation, the players, or the outcomes. But they do have a solid interest in you. Your group can be people who are *for you* so you can be better at being for *others*.

> **Tom:** Bob is a dad, and he deeply desired to be a good father. But he struggled with his anger, which his kids seemed uniquely gifted at evoking. Consequently, domestic life was stressful and contentious. As a father of eight, believe me, I felt for Bob when he confessed his problem to our group. After one particularly bruising family encounter, Bob determined to bring each and every incident to our group and allow them to hold him accountable. That simple exercise, over time, helped Bob modify his reactions at home and in the process changed his home life.

5. Small groups help us carry one another's burdens.

We all have responsibilities we accept and burdens we carry. Most times, we can handle them on our own, but inevitably we will hit difficult periods when we struggle with those same burdens and responsibilities. We can even become overwhelmed by some tragedy or a sudden multiplication of problems that are greater than our spiritual and emotional reserves. It happens to all of us. That's why Paul wrote, "Bear one another's burdens, and so you will fulfill the law of Christ. For if anyone thinks he is something when he is nothing, he is deluding himself" (Gal 6:2–3).

Paul teaches us that if we think we can handle our burdens on our own, we're acting foolishly. The law of Christ is to love and care for one another, bearing the burdens of life together.

> **Father Michael:** At Sunday Mass, even in a small parish, it just isn't possible or practical for people to know the burdens you're carrying. It's likewise impossible for you to know other people's struggles unless you are in a small group. Over the years, I have again and again seen the power of a small group when someone hits trouble or tragedy.
>
> One Sunday morning, word was brought to me that a parishioner, a college student, had died suddenly the night before. After morning Masses, some of the staff accompanied me to her parents' home. We were heartbroken by the situation but heartened by the scene we stepped into. Members of the parents' small group were already on hand, answering the door and the phone, preparing food, sitting with and praying over the grieving family members. It was an amazing scene of Christ followers carrying one another's burdens.

6. Small groups help us to believe in God's goodness when we struggle to believe for ourselves.

We find a very interesting story in the second chapter of Mark's gospel. Jesus returns to Capernaum, the town that served as the home base for his ministry. The last time he was in town, he had begun to gain a reputation as a healer and wonder-worker, leaving behind crowds of people who wanted to attract his attention and win his favor. He left because he learned in prayer that his Father had work for him to do in other towns. Now that he is back, word quickly spreads through the town, and crowds come out to hear him preach and teach. Mark writes:

> Many gathered together,
> so that there was no longer room for them,
> not even around the door,
> and he preached the word to them.
> And they came bringing to him a paralytic carried by
>   four men.
> Unable to get near Jesus because of the crowd,
> they opened up the roof above him.
> After they had broken through,
> they let down the mat on which the paralytic was lying.
> —Mark 2:2–4

Four men carrying a paralyzed man on a stretcher want Jesus to heal their friend, but they can't get near him because of the huge crowd gathered around him. At that point, they could have given up, deciding that it just wasn't meant to be. Perhaps saying to their friend, "We're sorry. We tried to get you to Jesus, but we can't do it."

They could have had that reaction, but instead they persevere, climbing up onto the roof. Made of mud and straw or clay tiles, it would have been possible to form an opening in the roof through which to lower their friend. Here's what happened: "When Jesus saw their faith . . ." (Mk 2:5).

Wait a minute, *whose* faith does Jesus see? He sees the faith of the paralytic's friends. He sees that they persevered to get their friend to him. As a result of their faith, Jesus acts, forgiving their friend's sins and healing his paralysis.

Ever notice that sometimes, maybe even *often*, it is easier to do something for someone else than it is for yourself? You can end up chipping in and helping out with someone else's home improvement project while neglecting your own house. You find yourself preparing food for a family experiencing a difficult time or undertaking yard work for an elderly neighbor that you would not bother to do for yourself.

Sometimes, when it comes to our problems, we are so much in the thick of them that we can't see the answer. But when we observe someone else's situation, we can so clearly see it, and often even quickly identify the solution. It is so obvious that they should take the job, break up with the boyfriend, sell the house. Likewise, it can be easier to have faith and believe for someone else than you do for yourself. At some point, we all struggle with believing in God's goodness, his power to heal, his willingness to bring us through a difficult or challenging period. We doubt that God really has the whole world in his hands (much less *our* world).

Given such scenarios, the firm faith of a friend can be a powerful support. This is another reason small groups are so important. We need others who can believe in God's goodness and power for us when we struggle to believe it for ourselves. Jesus can use their faith to accomplish something in our lives. Faith can be transferred like money between accounts. Likewise, God can use *our* faith to positively affect the lives of others.

Father Michael: Another sad story illustrates the point beautifully. AJ and Stephanie were new to our parish and to Baltimore, having relocated here for AJ's work. Stephanie took her first opportunity to join a moms' small group, as she was nine months pregnant and a first-time mom, looking for support, advice, and encouragement. She got quite a lot more. Days after giving birth, the baby suddenly, unexpectedly died. The parents were shattered, their faith in God's goodness shaken to the core.

Making a worst-case scenario even more tragic, it all happened during a heavy snowstorm, rendering it simply impossible for any of their friends and family from across the country to join them or help with the funeral arrangements. This is where the moms' group Stephanie had joined stepped up to help out and eventually handled everything. They contacted the funeral home, planned the liturgy, selected the music, and formed the only congregation at the Mass. In the absence of friends and family, they provided a reception, even offering a brief "eulogy." They carried their friend through tragedy, believing in God's goodness for her.

FOR REFLECTION AND CONVERSATION

1. Who are three to five key people you would ideally like to see step forward to support small-group life in your parish? Write down their names.

2. Which benefits of small groups listed in this chapter would these people find most compelling?

3. What benefits of becoming a parish of small groups do you find most compelling? How enthused would you be to share these with others?

Extra credit: Practice a two-minute elevator pitch for small groups based on what you have read in this chapter.

| 4 |

Recognizing the Benefits for the Pastor and the Parish Staff

Joint undertakings stand a better chance
when they benefit both sides.

—Euripides

Launching and building a small-group ministry takes work. In the beginning, it can be especially labor-intensive and deeply frustrating. In plowing the ground and sowing the seeds for an effective small-group ministry, you will hit many roots and rocks along the way. Often, as a result, parish staff and leaders give up too quickly or don't even invest the energy and effort needed to get started.

Scripture tells us we reap what we sow. And the principle of reaping and sowing tells us we reap *later* and *greater*. The fruit of our labor does not come right away but in a future season. The fruit also far surpasses our efforts. We receive so much more than the work we undertake or the resources we invest. Small groups absolutely pay off later and greater than your effort. So, we want to share with you *five* key benefits that you will enjoy as a pastor, a parish staff member, or other leader if you invest in planting a small-group ministry in your parish.

1. Groups provide an efficient, effective, reliable, and sustainable system of pastoral care.

From our own experience, we've come to believe that one priest can effectively care for no more than two hundred parishioners. Little wonder then that the average size of churches in this country is fewer than two hundred members. If the pastor, or even the pastor and the parish staff alone, must provide member care, then there is a lid on your parish's health and growth.

The fact is that clergy and staff cannot provide all the support for our members that they need, especially in a large, growing, or geographically wide parish. The other fact is, they don't have to. Building up a small-group program can efficiently and effectively provide for members' needs. Rather than having to call the church for a listening ear or a shoulder to cry on, small groups form the bonds that support people in times of struggle. As we mentioned in the last chapter, it is a place for members to share one another's burdens. When parishioners are willing to do that, it greatly reduces the demands they will place on staff and clergy. It spreads out the responsibility of member care to every single parishioner, dramatically increasing the number of people the parish can care for.

Small groups expand the *reach* of pastoral care as well as improve the *quality* of care. Small-group members are bringing their comfort and care to just one person, whom they already know at a personal level. Consequently, they can arguably extend that comfort and care further than the parish staff ever could.

Over and over again, we have seen how members care for one another in ways impossible for our staff. Groups have provided meals during times of illness, watched over and cared for one another's kids, helped out with medical appointments. Most important of all, many times we have seen group members rally around a group member at the time of their greatest need.

Father Michael: One of my most memorable moments came when I met with a family who lost a brother due to a sudden illness. They were in my office to plan the funeral liturgy, but interestingly, they had brought along their small group. I listened to and prayed with the group, but the family's grief was raw and my prayers felt hardly adequate for the tragedy we were confronting. If you are a pastor or church staff member, you know the feeling of helplessness and hopelessness in such moments. I wrapped the meeting up with a heaviness of heart for the situation, feeling as if I'd failed. As the group prepared to leave, one of the members grabbed my arm and said, "Don't worry about them. Our small group will surround them with care in these difficult days and walk with them in the months ahead."

While I still hurt for the family, I watched them walk away grateful for the power of groups and thankful that we had invested so much time and energy into them. As a pastor, it is encouraging to know that this quality of care takes place in our parish, as group members minister and care for one another. Such groups beautifully illustrate what it means to be the Body of Christ, knowing, loving, and caring for one another.

If you are a pastor or parish leader and have a compassionate, pastoral heart for people, encouraging others to provide the care you have always provided might seem counterintuitive, but hear us out. The best pastoral strategy is not necessarily investing one-on-one time with people who are hurting. Certainly, you should do that, when and where you can. As church leaders, it's important to keep our hearts attuned to the daily problems and special struggles people face. But it's also important to acknowledge you can't do everything for everyone.

We refer to the axiom "do for one what you can't do for all." This is an idea we adapted from our friend Pastor Andy Stanley. It refers to an approach in which pastors and parish pastoral staff do indeed provide pastoral care, *some* of the time for *some* of the people. But this is not just symbolic, it's not meant to relieve our guilt or make us look good. It's simply doing exactly what it says, providing for someone what you might like to but can't do for everyone. Essentially, the pastor models pastoral care to the parish.

2. Groups build unity in the Body of Christ.

We live in a generation and culture where church attendance is becoming less and less the norm. Past generations stayed connected to their local parish out of tradition, obligation, less geographic mobility, and greater trust of institutions. A respect for tradition has been lost. Attending church out of obligation was a waning practice before COVID-19 and has now almost entirely vanished. People are more than ever on the move, and trust in institutions is incredibly low across the board. Yet, the desire to connect with God and the hunger for genuine community remain. They lie deep in our souls. We cannot escape them.

When parishioners have a small group, they can experience that sense of community. They connect with other believers forming relationships that far outweigh the respect for tradition, the duty of obligation, or trust in an institution. Their bond to Christ's Church deepens as they develop a love and concern for other Christ followers. In a time when people are falling away or just walking away from the Church, small groups make it *more likely* they will stick around, with a stronger bond to the parish.

Building up small groups gives people what they are really hungering for—connection to Christ and connection to one another. And when a critical mass of people experiences this genuine unity and connection in an authentic way in a small setting, it builds unity in the larger parish. In our experience, it is often the case that small-group participation actually leads otherwise unchurched people back to Mass and gives them a greater appreciation for the Eucharist.

We do, however, offer a caveat to this step. For groups to build unity, it means we must be *intentional* about groups. It means we build a church *of* small groups (as we discussed in the last chapter). Otherwise, the parish runs the risk of creating a church within the church, the small groups become "holy huddles" for the true believers, and everyone else is automatically an outsider.

3. Groups make disciples.

Small groups are a key component in making disciples or students of Jesus Christ. They create an environment where members of our parish can routinely step out of their daily grind to evaluate their walk with Christ. Groups build into our members' regular schedule a time for spiritual reflection. They are a place where we can ask questions such as these:

- How is your heart? How is your marriage? How are your kids?
- What doubts or struggles do you have in your faith right now?
- How is your prayer life? Who are the unchurched family and friends you are praying for?

Aside from groups, where else are people going to be asked to reflect on these questions? Where else can people find a community of people who care how they are living and living out their faith? Asking and reflecting on our lives, in light of our faith, is how we grow as disciples.

4. Group members give more.

As evidence of the point above, we have found that small-group members give more of their time and money to the parish. Small-group members are far more likely to volunteer in the parish than those not in small groups; about two-thirds of our member-ministers (the parish volunteers) are in a group. And that's not all. Our financial officer, Brandon, did a comparison of people in groups versus nongroup members and found that the average group member gave double compared to the nongroup member in the offertory collection. This is consistent with what we hear from every parish small-group program we know.

But it's not just about how many parishioners are serving in the parish or how much money is raised. We believe, based on our experience in our parish, that participation in small groups grows givers and cultivates generous hearts. Literally, it changes hearts.

5. Groups will increase commitment to your parish's mission and vision.

As more people get involved in group life, growing as Christ followers, you will find more and more people committed to the mission and vision of your parish. That means when you move to launch fresh initiatives, propose new missions and ministries, or even kick off a stewardship appeal or capital campaign, you will find it much easier with a thriving small-groups program. It simply becomes easier to communicate goals, introduce changes, and take new directions. It means parishioners are *with you*.

FOR REFLECTION AND CONVERSATION

1. Which of these benefits is of most immediate need to you or your parish?

2. Which of the benefits most excites you?

3. What other benefits can you see small groups bringing for parish leadership?

STEP III
Build Your Team

| 5 |

Building Your Core Team

I can do things you cannot, you can do things I cannot;
together we can do great things.

—Mother Teresa

We now move to the third key step to developing a sustainable, healthy small-group ministry. Building your leadership team will take some effort and energy. If you are enthused about small-group ministry, you might be tempted to rush past this step or diminish its importance. Don't give in to that temptation! Without the right team, small-group ministry will flounder and fail, eventually fading away entirely. Inviting others into leadership, on the other hand, can create momentum to build a program with accountability to keep it healthy and strong. In this chapter, we want to share with you the key roles you will need to fill on your leadership team.

1. The Pastor

We start with the pastor, but ideally, or at least eventually, the pastor will not run the small-group leadership team or even serve on it. However, the pastor does play a key role in launching, sustaining, and growing a small-group ministry. The first way he can help is by simply being *for* the ministry and supporting the initiative. If the pastor makes known his support for small groups from the beginning, others will have the permission and space

43

to get on board. Just the presence of the pastor at early meetings powerfully demonstrates that small groups matter and are worth energy and effort.

Pastors also play an essential role in recruiting key leaders to give their time and energy to the initiative. Early on at Church of the Nativity, Father Michael carefully identified members of our parish to serve in leadership for our small groups. His personal invitation carried a great deal of weight. People with leadership gifts who had been on the sidelines stepped up to help at his request.

In addition to finding key leaders, the pastor shares his vision for small groups. At the initial meetings with leaders, the pastor can explain the reason small-group ministry deserves the investment of the parish and the benefits it will have for the congregation (see chapter 4). Eventually, the pastor speaks from the pulpit sharing this vision.

And last, but not least, the pastor must lead by example and get into a small group himself. If he invites people into a small group without being in one himself, then his preaching and promotion for group life will ring hollow. Also, getting into a group himself more or less eliminates any excuses from parishioners.

> **Father Michael:** Many times after preaching on small groups, people will come up to me and say, "I'll join a group when you do. Are you in a small group?" They expect me to say no, thereby giving them permission to ignore my invitation. When I can say yes, it shuts down their objections and opens them up to the idea.
>
> Besides all the other benefits of small groups, a basic benefit for me comes in gaining insight into what's really going on with parishioners and

how my weekly homily is landing in their lives. My life is so different from most of the members of the parish. My small-group experiences have kept me grounded in the realities of our community's culture, in turn improving the relevancy of my preaching.

I can understand that pastors may have concerns about getting into a group with members of the parish and sharing what's on their hearts. How about confidentiality? What about proper boundaries? One way to approach the problem is to carefully select who will be in your group and choose only people (men) you already know and trust. Also, let someone else serve as the leader so you don't completely dominate the group.

A second way to make a group work for you as a pastor would be to find a group outside of the parish. Join a group with other priests, such as an "Emmaus" group. Perhaps a group at another church or with people in another part of the country (via Zoom) could work. The point is that the pastor experiences small-group community so he can both truly experience the growth that comes from small groups and speak with conviction about the powerful benefits of groups.

2. The Small-Group Director

The small-group director (full- or part-time staff member or volunteer), together with the pastor, takes primary responsibility for the growth and health of small-group ministry and for setting goals and priorities. They help select and invite leaders onto the leadership team, set the agenda, and chair the meetings. The small-group director works with the pastor to make sure groups *align* with the mission and vision of the parish as well as reflect parish values. Taking responsibility for identifying small-group leaders, they also oversee their training and the launching of brand-new groups. If that sounds like a lot of work, it is. But notice, we said they take responsibility for those efforts, they don't actually do all those things themselves. They find good leaders to delegate those responsibilities and associated tasks.

In essence, the small-group director is the small-group "champion" in the life of the parish. Their number one job is to care about groups much more than anyone else, including the pastor. In fact, they will probably have to consistently remind the pastor and staff about the value of groups and work to keep them at the forefront of parish efforts.

Ideally, the small-group director will have a talent for connecting and communicating with leaders, encouraging and inspiring them regarding the ministry.

> **Tom:** I served as the very first small-group director here at Nativity. Like some of you, that was just one of my many jobs and "other duties as assigned by the pastor." I fell into it by accident and didn't really know what I was doing. We initially launched groups in an extremely modest way. Even so, it was a short-lived effort because I didn't understand that groups need constant maintenance. It became clear someone had to take ongoing and focused responsibility for them. It was also clear that I cared more about their success than anyone else on staff (including Father Michael, who cared a lot). So, I carved out time

from my schedule, stopped doing a lot of other things, started prioritizing meeting with our leadership team, and had one-on-ones with the group leaders. As our program grew, we were able to create a staff position.

3. Coaches

Coaches serve as the direct conduits from the leadership team to the small-group leaders. In forming a small-group ministry, you may be tempted to think this falls to the small-group director. But if the group director has to handle all the questions and concerns that come from group leaders, especially as the program is first introduced, it could be overwhelming, depending on how many groups you have. Also, having coaches in place will increase the care for group leaders just as groups increase the care for members of the parish. We'll take a closer look at coaches in the next chapter.

4. Data Coordinator

Our advice on this role comes from personal experience and pain. When we first launched small groups in our parish, we had people sign up for groups on bulletin boards in the lobby. It was an old-fashioned, labor-intensive exercise, involving deciphering people's poor handwriting and trying to figure out their real names and contact information.

Our frustration would continue for the next couple of years. As we set out to grow groups, we struggled to establish the baseline of exactly how many groups we really had and how many people were actually participating. It took months and months to collect the data, and often by the time we did, it was already outdated. It always felt as if we were chasing our own tails.

So, as you start out, identify the person on your team who will help you efficiently register parishioners for groups at your small-group launch. The data person will coordinate the technical side of the registration process for small groups, whether through texting, online registration, or however you decide to run the process moving forward. You want to find someone who has knowledge of and interest in the various platforms and technologies that now exist. This is a never-ending task, as people are constantly joining, changing, and leaving groups and as groups themselves are forming, reforming, and disbanding. Consequently, you are looking for someone who is a patient plotter.

Learn from our pain on this one. As non-tech, non-data people who just wanted to get people in groups, we didn't pay enough attention to the very practical details of data collection and maintenance. You can do better.

5. Prayer/Communications Coordinator

We go back and forth on whether this should be one role or two. For our purposes here, we will combine these functions into one.

We need prayer to launch and grow groups successfully. We need prayer to invite people into group life. And without the prompting of the Holy Spirit moving in people's hearts, the fruit of prayer, they will never accept the invitation.

The prayer coordinator creates a prayer plan for the success of the small-group launch as well as prayerful support moving forward. A daily email in the form of a brief devotional can be quite efficient and effective. Other ideas for a prayer plan might include a regular schedule of Eucharistic Adoration, asking the daily Rosary people or other prayer teams to remember small groups in their intentions, or making it an intention of the Universal Prayer at Sunday and daily Mass. The point is to cover the launch in prayer.

And then afterward, the prayer coordinator can help promote a spirit of prayer in groups and *for* groups.

The communications coordinator creates a communication plan to promote small groups in the parish. He or she will write copy for the bulletin and website, as well as create social media posts. Once groups are launched, the coordinator will take responsibility for ongoing communication. If you separate this role from that of the prayer coordinator, the communication coordinator will work closely with the prayer coordinator to communicate the prayer plan. Ideally, the communications coordinator will have good writing skills, be comfortable posting on social media, and be proficient in using various communication platforms.

As we wrap up this chapter, hopefully you can see that building a small-group ministry is a team effort. Start looking out for the talented parishioners to recruit for your team to help build your small-group ministry. Have faith that God has exactly the right people in mind to fill these roles. As scripture tells us, "For we are his handiwork, created in Christ Jesus for the good works that God has prepared in advance, that we should live in them" (Eph 2:10).

There are people already sitting in your pews who have been shaped by God to do the good work that is necessary for a small-group ministry to thrive. Rely on God, and you will be amazed at what encounters he will arrange.

FOR REFLECTION AND CONVERSATION

1. What is your reaction as pastor (or what will be the reaction of your pastor) to the description of the plan proposed in this chapter? Will it be embraced, or will there be reservations and objections? What will these be?

2. Who are some parishioners who come to mind when considering the roles that we've described?

3. Which roles will be easiest to fill? Which role will be most difficult to fill?

| 6 |

Understanding the Value of Coaches

Coaching is taking a player where they can't take themselves.

—Coach José Mourinho

In building your team, you will want to pay special attention to group coaches. So important are they that some larger churches pay their coaches. We have never been able to make that level of investment, and we would guess it is also out of reach for most other Catholic parishes. We mention this fact just to underscore the importance of coaches. The temptation will be to build a flat organization, and that would be a mistake. Coaches serve three very important roles.

Role 1

First and foremost, coaches serve as the principal point of contact between small-group leaders and the leadership team. They are a key link in the chain of command from pastor to the parish director of small groups and to group members, ensuring that everyone remains unified with the vision and mission of the parish.

Role 2

Coaches provide support and serve as a resource for group leaders in dealing with problems in their group (see chapters 17 and 18).

Coaches support group leaders by sharing with them grace and truth. Coaches give group leaders grace simply by their presence. Just the fact that someone is available to lend an ear, acknowledge their challenges, and in the process affirm and encourage them is definitely a grace. Coaches can provide group leaders with truth in the form of honest feedback in various ways. They can help group leaders clarify the problems they are really facing, allowing them to see the issue from a different perspective. By offering truth, coaches will provide insight into the situation and, when needed, advice on how to solve it.

Role 3

Coaches help make happen the spiritual journey that this ministry intends for our group leaders. As we will subsequently discuss, we want our leaders to grow closer to Christ as a result of their time leading groups. Coaches encourage them to connect the dots between leading a group and becoming a more fully devoted follower of Christ. Ideally, coaches help group leaders grow in their own prayer life and appreciation of the Eucharist while modeling Christian discipleship themselves.

To enable coaches to effectively fulfill these roles, there are four qualities we suggest are important for a coach to have. While nobody will have all of these attributes, the right candidates should at least have some of these. Seek coach candidates who do the following:

1. Value experience.

Ideally, they will have small-group experience, and in most Catholic parishes this will be a challenge. When we started groups, we didn't have anyone who had been in a small group previously, and it somewhat handicapped our initial efforts. If that is you, simply be aware of this challenge as you move forward. In your first few seasons, this will probably be an aspirational goal.

2. Find wisdom figures.

These are people who have common sense and good judgment. They are growing in their relationship with Christ and aspire to reflect his character. A good litmus test would be to ask yourself one simple question: "Would I go to this person with a problem, confident in their good counsel?"

3. Look for listeners.

As mentioned above, simply being present and listening to a small-group leader will be an important asset. You do not want a big talker who dominates the conversation. Instead, look for potential coaches who are willing to listen. It has been said there are two types of people in the world. There are those who walk into a room and say, "Hello, here I am." They want the attention. The second type of person says, "Hello, there you are." They take an interest in the people around them. That's the person you want.

4. Insist on shared mission and vision.

Find coaches who understand the vision, mission, and goals of small groups for your parish. Coaches need to be 100 percent on board with where the parish is going and what you are doing. They should be able to articulate it at least as well if not better than you.

We've learned that coaches are exceptionally strong and effective when they are working in pairs. Besides, it's practical and it is biblical. "The Lord appointed seventy[-two] others whom he sent ahead of him in pairs to every town and place he intended to visit" (Lk 10:1).

One other note: as the ministry grows, you will ultimately want to divide this responsibility by "affinity." Now that we have so many in small groups here in our parish, we organize our coaches so that we have guys coaching guys' groups, moms coaching moms' groups, young adults coaching young adult groups, and so forth.

So, where do you find these people with the qualities we've described? In your parish, you perhaps have managers and HR professionals who play a similar role in their companies or organizations. Their job is to listen to employees, keep them aligned with the mission of the business, and help them develop and grow. Some of them will not want to undertake the same work in their parish, which is totally understandable. Others, however, will welcome the opportunity to use their professional experience to serve the parish. Also, look for people who might actually be in the coaching world. Lots of parents have plenty of coaching experience with their kids' sports teams. Business coaching has exploded over the last few years, and you may have some personal development coaches who would work well in the role. The Holy Spirit tends to move and awaken us to the people he inspires to service when we start looking for them. As Jesus himself assured us, "Seek and you will find" (Mt 7:7).

FOR REFLECTION AND CONVERSATION

1. Do you think it is important to build a team of coaches for small-group ministry? Why?

2. Of the roles described, which one do you think is most important?

3. Which people come to mind when you think about finding coaches? Brainstorm a list, write down their names, and rate them in terms of interest and availability.

| 7 |

Finding the Leaders You Need

> If your actions inspire others to dream more,
> do more, learn more and become more, you are a leader.
>
> —John Quincy Adams

The success of a small-group ministry depends largely on the small-group leaders who direct and facilitate the groups. Small groups create an environment where people develop friendships and mutually encourage one another in faith. Without small-group leaders who have the knowledge, understanding, and wisdom to facilitate this environment, your groups run the risk of becoming unhealthy gossip centers or simply ineffective and superficial social circles. With the right leaders, they become powerful environments of transformation and life change.

Throughout this chapter we will share with you the qualities to look for in a small-group leader and dive deeper into their responsibilities. As we consider these qualities, we hope you will gain a greater vision and understanding of what healthy groups look like.

1. Look for small-group leaders who have a living faith in Christ, even if they are new to faith.

This might sound obvious, but there are many churchgoers and cultural Catholics who actually don't have a personal relationship with Jesus Christ and perhaps don't really believe he is the Son of

God. They are welcome to join our groups and be a part of our gatherings, just not to lead them. Group leaders do not have to be very far along in their faith journey. They can even be somewhat new to faith, but without a faith in the living Lord they will not be able to direct the group in a meaningful way.

2. Look for leaders who buy into the vision and mission of the parish.

If group leaders do not know and support the direction of the parish leadership, groups risk becoming environments where people evaluate and inevitably complain about the parish. In fact, such groups can even breed complaints through one complainer's gripes and grievances awakening and fueling others. This is the very reason some pastors avoid groups altogether in their parishes. On the positive side, when group leaders support the mission of the parish to make disciples and help people go deeper in their faith, they can keep their groups focused on that purpose and be fruitful.

3. Look for humble people, especially humble enough to be willing to learn and grow.

We want people who understand that they have far to go as they aspire to grow as fully devoted followers of Jesus Christ. People join groups because they recognize the gap between where they are and who God has created them to be. We have flaws in character to be addressed, blind spots to overcome, wounds to be healed, and outright rebellion that requires repentance. Group leaders cultivate the humility to know they themselves have these gaps. So, they will model for the group how to lean into the group content and see how they can grow personally, which creates an environment for growth.

Humility is also needed to grow in the skills required of a group leader, especially when leading a group for the first time.

They will face problems as a group leader (see chapter 17), as well as people who present special challenges (see chapter 18). Humble people understand that these are likely challenges and look to serve the group nonetheless. In addition, they seek help from their coach or parish staff when they know a problem is over their head.

4. Look for emotionally healthy people.

Humility and emotional health go hand in hand. Often the first people who step forward to serve are the "churchy church" people who, while well meaning, are not necessarily emotionally healthy. Emotionally unhealthy people serving as leaders will hijack the group, making it all about them. They will use the group as a platform to get attention for only their concerns and issues. On the other hand, emotionally healthy people see the groups not as all about themselves but as a place for interpersonal growth precisely by learning from one another. They step forward to lead the group *not* so they can be large and in charge but to help foster interdependent relationships, with a capacity to be vulnerable. Groups will certainly have people who lack emotional health, but they cannot be led by them.

5. Look for leaders who are likable.

Would you want to spend an hour and a half each week with this person? If the answer is yes, then they are probably a good candidate for leadership. If the answer is no, then you probably don't want them leading a group.

6. Look for people of growing faith.

These are people who walk the walk of faith grounded in daily quiet time, are fed on the Eucharist each week, and have a faith that is very practical and drives their daily behavior and decisions. They will be your very best leaders. Perhaps you will not find many of them at first, so this can't be set as a requirement. Consider it a bonus when you discover someone in this category.

This might strike you as a formidable list, suggesting a perfect kind of person. Actually, we're not suggesting anything of the kind. For our leaders, we're simply looking for growing disciples. So, what is it you are actually asking them to *do*?

Job 1: Leaders promote prayer in their groups.

The purpose of small groups is to create change and transformation so that we become more like Christ through the power of relationships. This means we invite God into the conversation. So, prayer is absolutely essential. Jesus said, "For where two or three are gathered together in my name, there I am in the midst of them" (Mt 18:20). The group leader ensures that the group gathers in Jesus's name.

In the group, people will share burdens and challenges. It is up to the group leader to encourage the group to turn to the Lord with these concerns. So, at the end of the meeting, or even in the middle of the conversation, the group leader helps the group pray about these concerns. That could mean that at a particularly heavy point, the group leader stops and says, "Alright, let's give this over to the Lord right now. Jesus, we place this problem, this issue, in your hands."

Before closing the meeting, the group leader should lift up all the concerns and burdens of the group in prayer, or the leader might ask each member to pray for challenges addressed and concerns raised in the group's discussion. And, of course, prayer is always an opportunity to not just give our burdens to God but also offer praise and thanksgiving for the good things happening in group members' lives.

There are many ways to promote prayer in the group. The point is to connect the dots between the conversation and prayer. Group leaders ensure this happens.

Job 2: Leaders facilitate "faith conversations."

> The disciples asked each other, "Were not our hearts burning [within us] while he spoke to us on the way and opened the scriptures to us?" (Lk 24:32)

This is perhaps the most fundamental or core role of the small-group leader. A small group can help shape an environment for conversation rooted in faith, which leads to life change, as in the experience of the disciples with the risen Lord on the road to Emmaus. We create this environment because we believe everyone in the group has something to offer and everyone in the group has something to learn from one another's faith. So, the group leader looks to include everyone and successfully invites them to share their faith-based thoughts. And that takes skill. It takes skill to know how to get the quiet person to talk and how to get the talkative person to stop talking. It takes skill to redirect the conversation back to matters of spiritual growth when the group has gotten into topics such as politics, sports, or fixing the problems of the world.

It takes skill to facilitate any discussion, but facilitating a "faith discussion" takes spiritual discernment to recognize where the Holy Spirit is leading the discussion, and that just takes practice.

Job 3: Leaders ensure space for mutual support and encouragement.

If a member is sharing concerns or burdens, the group leader will slow the conversation down and know when to allow time to focus on him or her. Group leaders provide space so that other members can support him or her without preaching or giving unhelpful advice. If a member is enjoying an accomplishment or celebrating some success, the leader likewise ensures the proper enthusiasm is extended.

Job 4: Leaders keep the group connected to the parish.

Small groups ideally happen outside the parish walls, usually in members' homes, which is great but it can begin to feel as if they are not parish-based ministries. Group leaders form the connection back to the parish so that the leadership team can keep a pulse on the group.

Group leaders keep connected to the parish in a few ways. They help the parish maintain the group's data and contact information, especially when they have an open space for new members. They keep connected by staying close to their small-group coaches always working to ensure good communication. Attending trainings and opportunities for ongoing learning are other ways to maintain the connection. And simply staying abreast of parish news and information is key.

Job 5: Leaders build commitment to the group through *shared* leadership and responsibility.

This is an especially big one. Leaders don't create followers. They create other *leaders*. Early on, let small-group leaders know that they should impress upon members that while they facilitate the group, *everyone* has responsibility for it.

Group leaders facilitate shared leadership by eventually identifying a co-leader. In fact, in recruiting small-group leaders, you might want to *start* by inviting *two* people to *co-lead* a group (for the same reasons we discussed the value of co-coaching in the last chapter). If unable to do that, encourage small-group leaders to find a co-leader as soon as possible. The co-leader will facilitate the group when the leader cannot attend. Often, they take responsibility for communication, reminding members about group meetings.

The group leader also invites members to take turns hosting the group and doesn't necessarily host every single meeting themselves. If the thought of serving together in a service project or enjoying a social outing arises, the group leader invites others to plan the event.

We have talked about the qualities and responsibilities of group leaders, but how do you recruit them? Simple, you ask them. Okay, but whom do you ask? You can always start with some of the obvious people or insiders at your parish. Write down some of the names of people who easily come to mind. They are the usual suspects. Start there, but make sure you don't *stop* there. Push yourself to go beyond the go-to individuals. As we say in our book *Tools for Rebuilding*, you want to "widen the gene pool" and find new people. On weekends, pay attention to parishioners who are regular attendees but have not been involved in the life of the parish, beyond Mass. Especially take note of the parishioners you like or who just seem like engaging people. Consider whom you would want to experience small-group life with because they will probably make a good leader.

Also, take a look at your Catholic school families or those in your program of religious education and youth ministry. Parents who are committed to their children's faith formation might have more interest in faith-sharing groups.

If you have any small groups currently meeting, invite members to help with the launch of new small groups by stepping up to lead a group themselves. In fact, this is our go-to plan for raising up new leaders now that we have an established small-group ministry.

Small-group leaders are absolutely vital to the health, well-being, and success of our small-group ministry. While it can be a challenge to find the right people, it is also a joy and a blessing to invite others into the work of this important ministry. You'll also be raising up a whole new core of parish leaders who are growing as disciples.

FOR REFLECTION AND CONVERSATION

1. Which qualities of a small-group leader do you find most helpful? Are there any you would add or subtract from the list?

2. What did you find useful about the description of the responsibilities of small-group leaders? How would you prioritize these responsibilities?

3. Right now, what steps can you take to find the small-group leaders you need to launch or expand small groups? Write out a job description for your small-group leaders.

| 8 |

Onboarding Small-Group Leaders

Teamwork is the ability to work together toward a common vision. It is the fuel that allows common people to attain uncommon results.

—Andrew Carnegie

Once you have identified and invited members of your parish to lead a small group, you will want to onboard and train them. In this chapter, we want to paint a vision of what that first meeting with leaders will look like. It's a critically important meeting because you are setting the foundation for small-group life in your parish, perhaps for years to come. As has been said, begin as you mean to go on.

The goal of the meeting is to relieve nervousness regarding their new responsibility and *bring clarity* to leaders about what you hope to accomplish in small groups. It's about getting them *excited* for what God will do in their groups and equipping them with the basics of how to *run* their group. As you can see, there is much to accomplish. What follows are ten points to cover in that first meeting. This is not an agenda per se but can help you form your agenda.

1. Thank them for being part of this exciting journey.

Let new leaders know you are grateful for the time and energy they are willing to invest in the parish and in building God's kingdom. Remind them that the Lord promises blessings for anyone who invests in his Church and that they will be blessed for their investment of time and energy in the parish. Your gratitude can come through your words as well as the environment you arrange for the meeting. Put some time and energy into the arrangement of the space you're meeting in, perhaps provide drinks and other hospitality when they arrive. Along with thanking them as a group, do your best to greet and thank everyone individually.

2. Share vision for small groups.

Ideally, this portion of the meeting will be presented by the pastor. If not, a key staff member should lead it. Take some time to talk about the value of small groups and why you are excited that they are taking this journey with you. Reflect on the benefits of small groups for inspiration (see chapter 3). Choose a few of the benefits and explain why they motivate you to bring small groups to the parish. Identify your favorite scripture verse about Christian community and group life and reflect on it with them (see appendix C). If you have small-group experience, tell your story and how groups have affected you.

Then, look ahead a year or more and cast a vision for what you see happening in the parish: the fruits of the small-groups program. Invite them to look forward to hearing stories of groups supporting one another, of members really tuning in to and turning on to their faith, stories of life changes. All of this will help new leaders understand that *you are* deeply committed to small groups and that you're in it for the long haul. This will strengthen *their* commitment and increase their excitement about groups.

3. Bring alignment among leaders (as best you can).

Group leaders are going to have their own ideas about what a group will look like, and every group will be a bit different. That's okay. It is an important value of groups that they take on different flavors and develop distinct styles. At the same time, we want overall consistency and some similar qualities to the experience of groups. Remind the leaders that the focus is on relationships and developing friends in faith, not necessarily about doctrine, scripture, or even initially about prayer. We like to say three things:

- We pray in small groups, but it is not a prayer group.
- We share our burdens, but it is not a support group.
- We read the Bible, but it is not a Bible study.

Rather, a small group is a mixture of prayer, support, and discussion based on scripture. As you will see, the other items on this list will also help align members.

4. Connect the small-group leaders with one another.

Small groups are all about relationships, so you will want this initial meeting to reflect that. While there might be a great deal of information to share, it would be a mistake to bring new leaders together and just talk to them, failing to give them a chance to connect with one another. In your agenda, provide the members with an opportunity to get to know one another. Let them exchange basic information about their family, work, and history at the parish. Have some fun: ask them to share an interesting or funny fact about themselves or their top three favorite movies. Give them a chance to express why they signed up to lead a small group and what they hope they will get out of it. If they're seated in a circle, give them discussion questions regarding group life, thereby mirroring exactly the small-group environment they'll be hosting.

5. Clarify the role of the small-group leader.

Take the previous chapter and create a small-group job description for your small-group leaders and thoughtfully review it with them. Let them know they will grow into the role over time; there is no reason to be intimidated or overwhelmed. Invite and encourage their questions about it. Also, describe the qualities you were looking for in a small-group leader. Tell them that you chose them because they reflect those qualities.

6. Reflect on the sample covenant you can find in appendix D and the commitments you are asking group members to make.

Small groups are sustainable because of shared values regarding what groups are about. To successfully onboard your new leaders, look closer at those values in the form of commitments. Use the commitments we'll address in chapter 10. In your meeting with leaders, the commitments will help bring alignment. They will have a clearer picture of what a small group should look and feel like in your parish.

7. Describe a typical small-group meeting.

See chapter 14 for a complete outline of our proposed format, which you can use or adapt. The point to emphasize with leaders is that you want to keep the format simple and that there is a definite beginning, middle, and end. Also, underscore the essential commitment to time limits regarding people's schedules. If a group goes over a few minutes, that is not a big deal, but if they keep running long, going significantly over the agreed-upon time, members will eventually stop coming.

8. Review the content plan for the first semester or season.

Group leaders will be very interested in (perhaps even anxious about) the focus and content of group reflection and discussion. We'll be discussing more on content in chapter 9.

Whatever material you choose for your first small-group series, share with leaders *why* you chose it and why you are excited that members of the parish will be covering it. Provide a brief overview of the content so they will know the arc of the series and where they are leading the group.

9. Help group leaders know whom they can turn to for support.

We want group leaders to appreciate that they are part of a larger community and not on an island. Make it very clear whom they can turn to with concerns or problems. This will be their coach if you have identified coaches. Acknowledge that whoever is supporting them may not have all the answers but will welcome their questions. For group leaders, more important than getting all the answers is knowing that someone has their back and that you are committed to learning with them.

10. Answer questions and set a check-in date. Pray.

Make time for questions and answers. As noted above, it's okay to say, "I don't know." If you have read this entire book, you can use it as a reference. If you are just reading this chapter as you prepare for your first meeting with leaders, well, you can say, "I haven't gotten that far in the book yet."

Also, set a date for a check-in meeting down the road a bit. This can be online or in person, but you will want to bring leaders together about halfway through the first season. At that meeting, you will give leaders a chance to share wins and celebrate their success. Then, give direction and provide tools on how to keep the group meeting together after that initial season or series of meetings.

Finally, close in prayer. Make the prayer a brief service of commitment and commissioning for leaders. If the pastor is in attendance (and he should be), he can extend a blessing over the group leaders, invoking God's grace and strength for their roles. Along with inviting God's blessing and favor over leaders, you will want them to walk away encouraged, uplifted, and inspired by the privilege they have to lead a small group. Let the final moment be a moment of gravitas, of weight and solemnity.

FOR REFLECTION AND CONVERSATION

1. Which of the above suggestions did you find most helpful? What would you change or tweak?

2. Set a date and time for your introductory meeting with small-group leaders.

3. Write out the agenda for your first meeting and decide who will cover which parts of the agenda.

STEP IV
Define the *What*

| 9 |

Determining Your Content

Content builds relationships.

—Andrew Davis

We can vividly remember the scene. About four weeks after launching small groups at our parish, and getting a thousand people to sign up, we were faced with the hard truth: we didn't really have a follow-up plan moving forward. Obviously, God was doing a great work among us, and we had to keep the momentum going in some way, but we were left thinking, "What's next? What direction do we give to groups that want to continue?" Our leadership team stared at one another blankly as we searched for a solution. We had expended so much energy getting groups started that we hadn't really thought about that question until that moment.

In the first years of our small-group experience, identifying content felt like a heavy burden in sustaining the ministry. Often the responsibility seemed unsustainable. While it still requires effort and energy, it is not the burden for us it once was. In this chapter, we hope to help you through some of the struggles of identifying content for your groups. However, we will begin with this paradoxical statement: content for groups is both vitally important and completely overemphasized.

Content matters because it sets the direction for the groups, and if they are effective, groups are setting the direction for the parish. Obviously, groups *need* something to get their conversation started and keep the conversation going. Solid content brings cohesion to the group and fuels discussion. It helps with quality control of the experience and will definitely lead to stronger groups. Poor or weak content—content that is uninteresting or irrelevant—will hurt the quality of your groups, not to mention waste people's time. So much of the small-group environment will be out of your control and beyond your influence. But you can influence and even direct the content groups use, to the extent you choose to. Content is key.

At the same time, content can become overemphasized. By that we mean you can find yourself in "analysis paralysis" when it comes to choosing content. Hours and hours of research can be expended trying to find exactly the right resources for your small groups to use. The exercise, and the underlying responsibility, can easily become overwhelming.

Over time, we learned that our groups didn't come for the content per se anyway. They came for the conversation and the relationships that the content stimulated. So, in choosing content we must remember it serves the group and not vice versa. Certainly, we want to choose content that is solid theologically and offers practical spiritual wisdom, but we don't have to overthink it. When it comes to content for small groups, you have one of at least five options.

1. Choose not to select any particular content at all.

This option is about letting small groups choose whatever *they* want to do. Perhaps give them some direction, with recommended websites or easily available curriculum, but allow them to be completely on their own. This is an option for sure, just not one we would suggest. In this approach, there will be little or no uniformity or overlap in group discussions from group to group and season to season, so the program is going to have less impact parish-wide. It also easily opens the door to groups going in the wrong direction.

2. Create a library of options.

Better, allow groups to choose from a library of curriculum that the leadership team has created and crafted. Research the many programs and resources that are available (there is a lot out there, much of it free). Groups can choose content based on affinity, liturgical seasons, faith formation programs, or scripture studies. For sure, your groups will be in different places at different times, but at least you are controlling the content and ensuring the quality.

3. Have all your small groups do the *same* content.

Better still, have your groups undertake the same content at the same time. This option does not mean an individual small group can't occasionally choose a curriculum or study that differs from the parish. If a dads' group wants to do a dads' study, or a couples' group wants to spend some additional time on a common challenge that has emerged in their discussion, that is always perfectly fine, as long as it's only for a season. But typically, you will want group content aligned so that your small groups are having the same or similar conversations; together, they are on the same journey.

Again, there is a wealth of content available, but you might want to be strategic about it as you plan out your year. An Advent or Christmas series, or a Lenten or Easter series, are obvious options, but how about a Eucharistic series in the spring or a series on family life in the fall? The list can go on and on.

4. Have your small groups do the same content based on the weekend homily.

The advantages of the previous point are actually strengthened in this approach, which we recommend for your consideration. How does it work? Well, in the beginning, for us, it was merely a matter of our small-group team meeting with the pastor at the beginning of each week to discuss the weekend readings and the homily's focus. Out of this discussion emerged the questions for group reflection, which we distributed via email, along with suggested readings for additional enrichment.

In more recent years, we've moved to a podcast format. After attending the Saturday vigil Mass, two members of our staff record and post (on our website and YouTube) their discussion, succinctly summing up the readings and message while suggesting possible discussion questions we have crafted for this purpose. We always end these podcasts the same way: "We hope our conversation starts *your* conversation." You can find copies of these podcasts on our YouTube channel if you want to see how we do them. Feel free to adapt them or just use them as they are.

5. Have your small groups do the same content based on your current "message series."

In our experience, this option is the most effective one. It is commonplace in many Protestant and Evangelical churches to offer sermon "series," multiple weekends with preaching focused on a single theme. But if you think about it, the practice makes so much more sense in our Catholic tradition, in view of the cycle of the Lectionary and the seasons of the liturgical year. It is about choosing a theme and, over the course of four or five weeks, exploring it at all weekend Masses, relying on the given readings of the day. The practice helps ensure that the whole parish hears a consistent message, which can have a powerful impact on its fellowship and unity. A more extensive explanation of our approach to message series can be found in our book *Rebuilt*. There, we also address the many objections raised to embracing message series, such as multiple preachers in a single parish.

In fact, the combination of a weekend message series matched with small-group discussion can profoundly move the whole parish in a single direction. Over the last number of years, we have shaped our Lenten message series as opportunities to do just that. Two years ago, we used our book *Seriously, God?* to look at the mystery of suffering. Our intent was that the series would be a breakthrough experience for parishioners when it comes to living in God's mercy and loving-kindness. Last year, we relied on another of our books, *Rebuilt Faith*, to spend time reflecting on the steps of discipleship, hoping it would take discipleship to a whole new level for many of our members. These efforts were remarkable events in the life of our parish, and our community was discernibly different afterward.

> **Father Michael:** On the weekend, parishioners sit in rows and I talk to them. In a small group, they sit in a circle, and it's their turn to talk. No matter how good the weekend homily is, by Tuesday everybody's forgotten it (and by Wednesday I have too). Small groups can keep the conversation going and focused. This practice will ensure your groups are moving in the same direction, going further, faster.
>
> I cannot overestimate the value of the whole parish hearing the same message on Sunday and then discussing it together during the week. It is nothing less than transformative. (For more on

this topic, please refer to our book *Rebuilding Your Message*.)

FOR REFLECTION AND CONVERSATION

1. Reflecting on the options outlined in this chapter, which direction do you lean for your parish? Why?

2. Who will be the person who selects content? Who is responsible for researching? Who makes the final decisions?

3. What will tie your process for evaluating the content? How will you measure the interest and effectiveness it generated?

| 10 |

Embracing Six Solid Commitments Essential to Small-Group Life

Decision making is easy when your values are clear.

—Roy Disney

In organizing a small group for yourself or a program at your parish, it is more than helpful to establish commitments that everyone accepts—it is essential. Solid commitments help create clear expectations, and simple ground rules keep groups functioning, focused, and fruitful. One reason pastors and parish leaders resist small groups is that they're inherently messy and can so easily get off track. We readily acknowledge that fact: they *are* messy and quickly *do* get off track. Groups can't be controlled, but they can be guided. When clear commitments are established from the first, groups more reliably function in a healthy manner.

If you are leading or launching groups, do yourself and your group members a favor and establish the basic commitments you will all honor moving forward. Your list of commitments should support the reasons you are doing small groups and the outcomes you hope they will accomplish. Whatever other commitments you agree to, make sure you include these indispensable six.

1. Show up.

Really? Of course, it seems like a given, but if left unspoken, members will inevitably, and then increasingly, not show up. For small groups to be successful, members need to specifically commit to actually being present and lend the gathering their full and active attention and participation.

We know that while most people have the best of intentions, skipping the group for other priorities will be a creeping and consistent temptation for members, even when they find value in the group. Members will absent themselves for all kinds of routine reasons: a doctor's appointment, a special project at work, or kids' sports programs. And sometimes it just comes down to running out of time or energy.

This particular problem is nothing new. Apparently, the early church faced the same challenge. The author of Hebrews wrote, "We must consider how to rouse one another to love and good works. We should not stay away from our assembly, as is the custom of some, but encourage one another" (Heb 10:24–25).

> **Tom:** In full disclosure, I find this to be the most challenging aspect of small-group life. With eight kids and a busy work schedule, I struggle to maintain my commitment to my group. I greatly value the time I spend in the group and yet typically find myself weighing whether or not to go as the meeting time approaches each week.

Strong and healthy small groups have members who make a commitment to showing up and honor it above other obligations and activities. Part of this commitment should be agreement on what constitutes legitimate absences: illness, weddings and funerals, out-of-town travel, and other obvious reasons that can be acknowledged.

> **Father Michael:** For sure, we want to nuance this. No group is ever going to have perfect attendance, and you can't expect it from your parishioners. But persistent and egregious absence cannot be ignored. At our parish, we have gone so far as to ask people to step down from group membership or at least take a break because of repeated absences. We do so gently, discreetly, and with charity.
>
> Typically, if this commitment is firmly and clearly agreed upon as the group is formed, or when others join, there are no hard feelings if someone is called out for their spotty or inconsistent attendance. They know that participation is that important to us, being foundational to the whole program. Why? Because small groups are all about relationships, and relationships only grow and develop over time, when we are *present* to others. Presence is essential. So, whether a group meets in person or on Zoom (an increasingly convenient and completely appropriate option for many), members must commit to showing up and being present to keep the relationships going and growing.

2. Promise to maintain absolute confidentiality.

We want our small groups to be places where people feel safe to share what is going on in their lives. In order for the group to be a safe space, members need to know that what they say will not be repeated elsewhere: what's said in group should remain in the group. When people get comfortable and trust is built, some very sensitive topics might come up. We've heard members share struggles with infidelity, alcohol abuse, addiction to pornography, serious family drama, and more. It is an incomparable strength of small groups that those issues can be shared without judgment or the risk of disclosure. So, confidentiality is absolutely essential.

The commitment to confidentiality limits the temptation to gossip or the danger of unintentional disclosures about group discussions outside the group. Scripture is pretty clear about the problem of gossip and how it will destroy community and fellowship. "One who slanders reveals secrets, but a trustworthy person keeps a confidence" (Prv 11:13), and "No foul language should come out of your mouths, but only such as is good for needed edification, that it may impart grace to those who hear" (Eph 4:29). According to James, "If anyone thinks he is religious and does not bridle his tongue but deceives his heart, his religion is vain" (Jas 1:26).

Whereas lack of attendance should be handled slowly, gently, and with an understanding of someone's circumstances, indiscretion—especially when it descends into gossip—needs to be dealt with clearly and firmly. And it must be addressed *quickly*, before damage is done and hearts are hurt.

When it comes to confidentiality, we do acknowledge its limits and the necessary nuances. Confidentiality is not synonymous with the seal of Confession. Outside the groups, we acknowledge that members may process what was discussed with a spouse if they are married. In those cases, we ask them to disclose only the general scenario and the broad circumstances, not the details or particulars, and never names. Any further discussion should be strictly avoided. Another exception to blanket confidentiality is an obvious one. If something is shared in the group that by law must be reported to authorities, then confidentiality doesn't apply. Likewise, if someone's life is in danger or self-harm is threatened, then that would be a reason to break confidentiality as well. When training group leaders, clearly identify the appointed staff person to whom they should reach out if these kinds of situations arise. These are extreme cases and, hopefully, extremely rare, but we do acknowledge the possibility.

The circumstances to break confidentiality will be rare, while a deep, shared commitment to confidentiality among group members can actually pave the way to intimacy and transparency. In an environment of absolute privacy, more personal, sometimes profoundly personal, information can be shared, leading to life-changing conversations.

3. Be growth-oriented.

The purpose of joining a small group is simple: to become more like the person of Jesus Christ. Scripture says, "For those he foreknew he also predestined to be conformed to the image of his Son, so that he might be the firstborn among many brothers" (Rom 8:29).

None of us has been perfectly conformed to the character of Christ. Nor are we fully formed disciples; rather, we are in the process of *becoming* more like Jesus. We are on a spiritual journey, hopefully acknowledging the gap between who we are and who God has created us to be. In groups, we're committed to closing the gap; that's the growth we're aiming for.

A commitment to being growth-oriented means we have permission, at times, to lovingly challenge one another. We can ask uncomfortable questions or at least questions that can make us pause and think.

A growth-oriented focus is very useful for keeping small-group discussions from going in the wrong direction. It helps avoid the conversation descending into politics, sports, or social gossip. The purpose of a group is not to provide commentary on current events or solve the problems of the world (or even the problems of the parish). In most groups, those conversations will inevitably happen, but the commitment to being in a small group is about solving the problems of the heart. So, when the discussion becomes misdirected, *then* a group leader can gently say, "How does this land in *your* life?" or "How does this challenge *you*?"

The commitment to being growth-oriented means we can challenge one another but also that we commit to encouraging one another. Truett Cathy, the founder of Chick-fil-A, once asked, "What is the tell-tale sign that someone needs encouragement? How can you look at them and know they need to be encouraged?" And then, after a dramatic pause, he would answer his own question, "They're breathing." We all need encouragement, especially in our faith. As the verse from Hebrews, previously referenced, states, "We must consider how to rouse one another to love and good works" (Heb 10:24).

4. Respect one another.

All of us are most comfortable with like-minded people who share our worldview. So, those are the friendships and relationships we tend to invest in. It's not the same in a small group. When you get into a group, you will discover different opinions and divergent views, perhaps in striking contrast to your own. At the same time, as we mentioned earlier, people will share prevailing faults and past failures, and that can be surprising.

And then there is the simple fact that people can be in very different places from one another on their spiritual journeys. Some people are biblically literate, but many cradle Catholics are not. Others have had a formal Catholic education and are well grounded in their faith, with a solid appreciation for the sacraments. And still others are new to their faith and largely unformed in it. There are parishioners for whom their faith finds expression in social justice issues or a commitment to pastoral care for the sick. Many are more attracted to the liturgy and ritual of our faith, or perhaps the history and traditions of the Church. Small groups will bring together all kinds of people who otherwise would never have connected. The point is that groups have power precisely because they bring a diverse group of people together, but only if *respect* for one another characterizes the group culture.

How does respect for one another play out in a group? To begin with, it means *listening* to one another speak. When someone else is speaking, we listen best by looking at them, making eye contact, and clearly taking interest in what they're saying. But respect for others might also mean knowing proper boundaries.

> **Father Michael:** I was in a guys' group where one of the members found himself going through a very messy, very ugly divorce, which, of course, he brought to the group. We listened to him, commiserated with him, and prayed over him. That first night was all about him, as it should have been. But as the divorce dragged on, becoming mutually and deeply destructive for both parties and, tragically, their children, it inevitably dominated the discussion. Every week became an update on the drama and our ongoing attempts to console our friend.
>
> Our small group was not prepared to provide the legal assistance and psychological support that the situation demanded. As a consequence, our meetings were increasingly uncomfortable and unproductive. Week by week, guys just stopped coming, and eventually the group disbanded.

Respect for one another means we don't excessively burden others with personal problems. At the same time, it means it's not our job to "fix" others or tell them what to do. If we do have pertinent and helpful advice, respect for others means that we ask permission to share it with them. We say something along the lines of this:

- Hey, can I give you some advice I have learned from my experience?
- Mind if I offer you a little feedback based on what I heard from your story?
- Thank you for sharing. I have a couple of thoughts on how to improve the situation and am happy to offer them when you're ready to hear them.

> **Tom:** "Bull in the ring" is a football drill. One player stands in the center of a circle as the coach calls out the name of one of the other players who make up the circle. That player in turn shouts "here" and then hits the guy in the center, who eventually takes hits from every angle, thus he's the bull in the ring. It's a good football drill aimed at always being prepared to take any kind of hit on the field. But it is decidedly not a good experience in a small group.
>
> One of the worst experiences in group life can come from sharing your struggles with the simple hope of getting something off your chest in a safe space. But instead, you end up feeling like a bull in the ring as everyone comes at you with *their* advice on how to fix *your* problem. There is a time for offering counsel, but when a whole group starts giving advice, it increases your burden rather than

lessens it. Often it comes from a lack of skill at showing respect for someone and their problems.

Respect says I'll give you advice *when* it is helpful and only *after* you are ready to hear it. Romans puts it this way, "Let love be sincere; hate what is evil, hold on to what is good; love one another with mutual affection; anticipate one another in showing honor" (Rom 12:9–10). Respect shows honor to others and makes our love sincere.

5. Be authentic.

One of the challenges of life is that we have to *be on* so much of the time. We have roles to play at work or school, among neighbors and friends, and even at home. Our societal conventions underscore this need. When people ask us, "How are you doing?" in a social or professional setting, it is meant as a common courtesy and nothing more. The near-universal answer, "I'm fine," confirms the point.

Social media exacerbates this need to project a preferred image. Think about it: what you see and learn about your friends and family on Instagram or Facebook is their *very best version* of themselves, their highlights. And what they're learning about you is likewise filtered.

That's okay. Even Jesus said to be careful about whom we share our life with when he warned about casting pearls before swine in Matthew 7:6. In other words, you can't open your heart to everybody or just anyone; you need to be discerning. But that also means it's even more important to have a safe place to be honest and authentic, warts and all.

We want our small groups to be places where members can truly be known for who they are. But we have to admit that being authentic often takes some time to get to know others and build trust. When achieved, what does it look like? It means not putting on airs about social status or intellectual posturing. It means not downplaying problems, or sidestepping the real challenges you face, and the actual faults and failures you've accrued. It means not turning the conversation to frivolous topics to avoid serious ones. It means being transparent.

Authenticity comes from sharing struggles but also celebrating the good things happening in our lives. A promotion at work, a marriage in the family, and the birth of a child are all important topics for discussion in the group. Share your testimony of the good work God has done for you and the favor you have found before him.

Father Michael: One of our group members, Mark, wrote this to me:

> From the first moments of my first men's small group, I finally realized I was not alone—that my problems, my shortcomings, and my sins were no more complex or uncommon than those of the men sitting around me. That day, I met a group of very strong guys, loving husbands, wonderful fathers, great leaders, and humble servants who give back: all flawed like me and facing challenges, some big ones, some small, and all very, very real for them. Like me, they didn't know how to solve them alone and on their own but knew there was something greater that pulled us together. Some had learned great tools, had weathered challenges, that others could use. Some just had wisdom we all valued.

It has been almost seven years since that first day, and we are still together, not just in our small group but also now as true friends and brothers who, together, have dealt with some of life's greatest challenges: family members passing, severe illness, troubled teens, children becoming adults, and job losses. But we have also shared many joys: new jobs, graduations, marriages, and births.

Scripture puts it this way: "Therefore, putting away falsehood, speak the truth, each one to his neighbor, for we are members one of another" (Eph 4:25).

At the end of the day, authenticity means speaking the truth of our hearts—the good, the bad, and the ugly—because we are members of one family of faith. It means speaking from the heart as well as the head.

6. Share leadership and responsibility.

As we've already discussed, in small groups we intend for members to *share* the leadership and responsibilities of the group as quickly as possible. When members feel personal responsibility for the group, and when they're exercising leadership in the group, they are much more likely to maintain their commitment to the group. In fact, shared responsibilities can actually strengthen their commitment.

This is why meeting in homes (and *not* at church) can be so helpful. While on the surface it can look like an obstacle to getting people into group life (and initially it always is), once people host, they have a greater connection to the group. It's hard not to show up for the group when it is being hosted in your home, and likewise it's sort of impolite not to attend a gathering in someone else's home. A meeting at a member's house is going to have a completely different feel; it will be a different experience than meeting in the church hall. To overcome the inevitable pushback, establish low expectations about what the setting needs to be (a backyard or club basement works just fine) and what preparation is required (it's not a meal or a party; bottled water is just fine).

One way we have found to motivate members to host is to assume they will. Asking, at the end of the meeting, who is willing to host the next one is always an uncomfortable moment (resolved only when someone finally feels enough guilt to volunteer). Instead, establish a schedule for each semester or season. Give them a deadline to get back to you with any dates they are unable to host. Most members will go with the group and allow you to open their homes.

Another way we promote leadership and responsibility is by telling members to let *everyone* know when they can't attend. The group leader is not the teacher or manager. So if a member is going to miss a meeting, don't text or email the *leader*; rather, text or email the *group*.

Shared leadership and responsibilities also mean others may take on a specific or special role in the group. If there is a desire to get the group together for a service project or social gathering, then someone other than the leader can take control of that special event. Another member might take the communications role and remind the group of when and where they are meeting. As you move forward in your group life, always keep in mind the option and opportunity of shared leadership.

This commitment also means the health of the group is everyone's responsibility, not just the group leader's. So together, the group creates a culture of showing up, confidentiality, and being growth-oriented, respectful, and authentic. It is also the group's role to hold one another accountable to those commitments as much as possible.

Those are the six commitments we have found helpful in our groups. You can use them as they are, modify them, or establish others if you decide. The point is that it's very important to have an established set of commitments. You might even write out a formal covenant that group members agree to sign (see appendix D). It will set the tone and direction for what you want small groups to be in the life of your parish and what you want your parish to be because of healthy small groups.

FOR REFLECTION AND CONVERSATION

1. Of the commitments listed, which do you consider most help-ful? Most important?

2. Are there additional commitments you would add?

3. What do you think are the best ways to communicate group commitments to group leaders and members?

| 11 |

Pausing

Nothing was ever as effective as a rightly timed pause.

—Mark Twain

In scripture, the Psalms are a collection of diverse prayers, praises, songs, and hymns. But again and again, the word *selah* can be found in the original Hebrew. *Selah* means to pause, as in stop for a moment and take a breath. Often, it comes after the psalmist has given expression to strong emotions before God.

We don't suggest for a moment that anything we have offered so far is deeply profound, but maybe you are experiencing various emotions in view of it all. Perhaps you might feel overwhelmed by the work that goes into building a small-group ministry. Maybe facing the challenges it entails and the opposition it might generate leaves you somewhat perplexed. But you are now more than halfway through the book. As you hike up the mountain of this project, take a minute to celebrate the progress you are enjoying.

Selah. Pause. Take a breath. Relax your shoulders. Remind yourself that this is all the work of God. Pray:

Heavenly Father,
you have given us the opportunity
to build a small-group ministry in our parish.
Thank you for the privilege of helping people
experience true Christian community and life change

through their small group.
We are grateful to you for using initiatives and efforts
to bring more of your grace into the world.
We offer everything we do to you
and trust you will use them for your glory.
In Jesus's name, I pray.
Amen.

STEP V

Launch Your Groups

| 12 |

Getting Started

Do not despise small beginnings
for the Lord rejoices to see the work begin.

—Zechariah 4:10 (NLT)

We now move to step 5: launching new small groups. In this chapter, we want to help you determine what your goal should be for the number of groups you will launch. Your first decision is a critical one: whether you want to "beta test" (just getting one or two groups going as a trial run) or launch a parish-wide program. In this chapter, we are going to look at the modest approach. Then in the next chapter, we will reflect on launching groups for the whole parish.

If you are just starting a small-group ministry at your parish, it's likely that most of the leadership has never had a group experience. So it makes sense to set a small goal. This modest approach could be a major win for a season if it is aimed at launching a process of growth.

> **Tom:** A friend of mine, Dan, a very successful businessman, shared with me his team's process for setting goals, introducing new initiatives, and managing growth for his company. When launching something new, they go through three basic

iterations. The first goal is to simply get it started, in whatever simple way they can. That's a win. Once started, they look to improve the exercise and add more people who will use the product or program, looking to expand it through addition. Then, in the third round, they think in terms not of addition but multiplication, to grow the project substantially.

This has been our experience with small groups. We started with just two groups in our first year. The next year, we invited a slightly wider circle of people to give groups a try. As a result, we added five more groups to our ministry and about fifty new people.

If you are in the first iteration of launching groups, then your goal for the year ahead will be to simply get groups started. Begin with just a few leaders and a few groups. Set a timeline for how long the groups will meet—somewhere from about six to nine months. The important thing is that the effort has a beginning, a middle, and most importantly, an end. Let group members know that the goal is to experience small-group life so eventually they can all share the experience with others. Your hope is that members of the group will step up to lead *other* groups in the next season or semester. Use this first experience to learn what it is like to be in a small group and run a small-group ministry.

If you are in the second iteration of groups, think about widening your reach. You may want to target the volunteer ministers in your parish. Perhaps starting with the families in your religious education program, your parish school community, or the daily Mass-goers would be fruitful. Identify people who are already involved in or committed to the parish who might be primed for an invitation to join a group. These are the very people who can serve as group leaders when you launch the program to the parish.

Again, do this for six to nine months. If you are approaching the third iteration, then it's time to launch to the whole parish. This is where you move from being a church with small groups to a church of small groups. Here you share with the entire parish that it is your goal to get everyone in a small group. This means planning a launch weekend, which we will discuss in chapter 13.

Whatever stage of getting started you're in, set a goal for the number of groups and the number of group members you're aiming for. Make that number realistic, but be bold, set an uncomfortable goal, and take a risk. Realistic means you *can* achieve it; risky means you don't necessarily know *how*. You will need to expend extra energy and effort, and you will definitely need God to show up too.

That's our suggestion for the process. But if God is encouraging you to go bigger, listen to God instead of us.

FOR REFLECTION AND CONVERSATION

1. Where are you in the process of launching groups?

2. What is a realistic yet risky number of groups and group members that you want to achieve in the season ahead? What other goals do you have for the next six to nine months with groups?

3. When it comes to getting groups started, what else do you hear God saying to you right now?

| 13 |

Launching to the Parish

Begin with the end in mind.

—Stephen Covey

If you are ready to launch small groups for your whole parish, congratulations! In this chapter, we will set you up for an effective weekend. What follows are the eight major factors for success.

1. The Date

Lock in the date that will serve as your launch weekend. On this weekend, everything, or almost everything, about the weekend experience at the parish will invite and lead people to take the step of getting into a small group. You will want to communicate to everyone on your small groups' team, as well as your entire staff, the importance of this weekend. This is an "all-call" weekend, and you need every team member's participation at *all* Masses.

Our first suggestion would be to choose a weekend in the winter season between Christmas and Ash Wednesday, ideally a week or two before Lent. That's because Lent is absolutely the very best time to launch small groups in your parish. Why? People in the pews instinctively want to do "more" in terms of going deeper in faith for the season, and you can present groups as the perfect way to provide the more they're looking for.

If you decide against a Lenten launch, and your community is like ours, choose a time in the early fall when people are home from summer vacations and school is back in session, but not too close to the holidays. On the weekends leading up to the launch, you will want to let people know the special weekend is coming. Invite them to think about joining a group. Do this to soften people's hearts and change their minds toward the idea of participating.

2. Style, Schedule, and (Most Critically) Location

Earlier, you identified the leaders who will help you lead, but now you need to get into the details of when and where they will be meeting. Reach out to each of your leaders and communicate the basic information concerning the group:

- Who is the group for? Is it an open group or one based on affinity?
- What day and time will they meet?
- Where will they meet? An in-person location or on Zoom?

You will need all this information in advance of your launch weekend so people can easily identify their preferred groups.

In this step, you will have to decide whether you will open up your campus for groups to meet. Admittedly, this can be a hotly contested issue. In many parishes, "real estate" can be at a premium; at others, there is simply no space available for an additional program. Besides, on-campus meetings will require at least some additional staff or volunteers to open up, set up, and clean up. Additional staffing might be necessary at highly desirable times when groups would be most likely to meet: evenings and weekends.

Think about this: the purpose of groups is to get people to connect "life on life." Through groups, we want parishioners to see that their faith life is not just limited to coming to church on the weekend. Instead, we live out our faith *in* our life. Meeting in homes, offices, or coffeehouses powerfully underscores this point. And if we limit small groups to meeting only in our church building, we dramatically limit their ability to grow. The usefulness of groups meeting outside of church is that they are not limited by our space.

On the other hand, we know it can be a challenge for some people to take twin steps of both joining a group *and* going to a stranger's house. And it can be seen as an even bigger challenge to welcome strangers and new friends into one's own home. This, in itself, can be the deal breaker for many parishioners. Besides, you can powerfully underscore your commitment to small groups in the life of the parish by opening your parish facilities to groups. So, what to do?

Here's how we have managed that tension. When we launch new small groups, for limited commitments like Lent, we do open up space in our parish for groups to meet. We use our religious ed classrooms, trading comfort for convenience. We do this at certain select times in the week that do not conflict with other parish programs, can be accommodated by the staff or volunteers involved, and make sense strategically for people's schedules. But this arrangement is limited to Lent each year. After the Lenten season, if the group wants to continue meeting, and hopefully their experience would make that desirable, they will have to identify a space of their own to meet. Of course, we do help group leaders figure out that plan for the future.

Another option to consider will be online groups. Pre-COVID-19, we did not have many (as in any) online groups. In fact, to tell the truth, no one ever considered it. But now, Zoom is an established, often-preferred mode of meeting in the post-COVID culture and, as a consequence, online and hybrid groups make up a small but not insignificant percentage of our groups. We would certainly advocate having groups online if you have someone willing to lead them. We admit a predisposition for in-person small groups but acknowledge that Zoom is a mighty attractive alternative for its convenience factor alone. Also, Zoom groups are a great way to stay connected to remote parishioners. And they can very effectively serve as an accessible (and therefore attractive) "front door" for those not totally sold on participating in small groups.

3. Data and Registration

Once you have the information you need from group leaders, you will want to load the information into your database or the software you are using. Make sure the registration team is crystal clear on *how* they want people to sign up. Having tablets or laptops available immediately following Mass during launch weekend, and staffed with computer-literate volunteers, will effectively encourage registration.

Think through these logistical issues as carefully as you can to make it as easy as possible for parishioners, even technologically challenged parishioners, to sign up. Give yourself some grace, though. You will probably not think of everything, and hopefully you will be able to laugh at whatever you didn't get quite right. Trust us, we had to learn to laugh at a lot of things!

4. Content and Resources

We have already reflected on the selection of content (chapter 9). But here we're referring to making sure you have the resources you will be distributing ready to go on your launch weekend. Not to put too fine a point on it, but the easiest win here is focusing on a single book, at least for your initial small-group experience. A single theme focused on a single book is easier for you to promote and easier for parishioners to understand. And here's a tip: if there is any way you can do it, give the book away. That's right, *give the book* away for free to anyone who signs up for a group. No kidding, people love free, and the giveaway works. If you can find a way to fit it into your budget, do it. If not, perhaps you can underwrite the cost, giving it to them at a discount. Certainly, from a budget standpoint, that would not be a sustainable plan moving forward, but a giveaway or deep discount could powerfully kick-start your program.

Identify the place where people can sign up for a group and pick up their book, a place that is not only easy to find but also hard to miss. During the first year we launched groups, we erected a tent in front of the church. Parishioners had to walk through the tent to get into church and, after Mass, back out to the parking lot. The group sign-up and giveaway book program was located in the tent, and everyone had to pass the books twice. The effort was very successful in a way it probably would not have been if people had to go looking for the books or had to purchase them. Think through those logistical details shaping an orderly process that creates excitement for groups.

5. Ministry Support

As we said, this is an all-hands-on-deck weekend. You will want to ask staff and, of course, the small-group leadership team to be present throughout the weekend—at *all* the Masses. Identifying themselves with colorful T-shirts, lanyards, or some other distinctive garb, they are your sales force, available to answer questions and invite friends and acquaintances to join a small group. Your ministry support team is all about one-on-one asks. If nothing else, the presence of a team of people excited and inspired by the prospect of a small-group program in your parish can generate interest and enthusiasm. The excitement will be attractive to prospective members.

6. Marketing and Communication

You will want to festively decorate the outside of your church and your lobby so that parishioners are reminded as they arrive that something special is happening this weekend. Balloons are an inexpensive way to communicate this, suggesting a festive and fun environment. If possible, create some striking, eye-catching signage or hang banners in hard-to-miss locations.

7. The Homily

> **Father Michael:** In preparing my weekend homily, I always try to answer three questions in advance. When it comes to the parishioners:
>
> - What do I want them to *know*?
> - What do I want them to *do*?
> - How do I want them to *feel*?

Sometimes, answering those questions can be challenging, but on a small-group launch weekend, it should be very easy. We want them to know about the value of Christian community and having friends in faith. We want them to join a small group, and we want them to feel inspired that joining a group will be an effective support to their faith journey.

Prepare your homily so that it inspires and influences people to sign up for a small group. You may even want to put your cards on the table at the beginning of your message: "As you can see, this is our small-group launch weekend, so I am going to do my best to convince you to join a small group for this Lent."

In the homily, paint the picture of how a small group will assist them in their week-to-week lives while helping to bring their faith to the next level. People are attracted to vision; vision motivates them to step up and get involved. So, share the vision of the difference small-group life will make in their lives. Let them know how God will use them to help others grow in faith too. As mentioned earlier, make sure you emphasize that no matter how advanced in your faith, you have something to *learn* from others, and no matter how new you are to faith, you have something to offer others. At the same time, underscore that groups are not just for the faithful few; they are not meant to be "holy huddles" for the pious and the prayerful, nor do they require any background in scripture or theology. Groups are for everyone.

Finally, make sure you are crystal clear on the one thing they need to do to get into a group. Don't give them complicated instructions; rather, provide just a few simple steps such as "text us" or "stop by the information table in the lobby after Mass."

If the ministry support team is your ground game, your homily is their air cover.

8. The Follow-Up

After someone signs up for a group, they should be contacted in a timely fashion and *thanked* for signing up. This can be as simple as an automated email that you draft in advance. Whatever the form, it should let them know that their small-group leader will be contacting them with details for the group. The small-group leader then needs to follow up promptly. Along with that specific email to people who signed up, you will also want to send a generic email or postcard to the whole parish during that week. In this communication, again thank those who signed up for a small group, in a general way, and extend an invitation to everyone else to sign up now.

The next weekend, celebrate the launch as a success, even if you were hoping for greater results. Mention it at Mass, again thanking those who signed up for taking this significant step of faith. What gets rewarded will get repeated, and your gratitude will plant a seed for members in the community who did not get on board this time to join next time. Shape the narrative that this is now an established part of parish life moving forward and an irresistible opportunity for everyone.

FOR REFLECTION AND CONVERSATION

1. Decide on a launch-date weekend that works for the team, respects the parish schedule, and is strategically advantageous.

2. Review this chapter. Decide who will own the specific responsibilities.

3. Write down any other thoughts you have on planning your launch weekend.

STEP VI

Serve Your Groups

| 14 |

Meeting as a Group

For a community to be whole and healthy,
it must be based on people's love and concern for each other.

—Millard Fuller

Congratulations! You have now made it to the final steps: launching, growing, and sustaining small groups in your parish. This is what it is all about—getting people into groups. What is *first* when it comes to intention is usually *last* in execution, so congratulations!

In this chapter, we will look at a typical small-group format we use at our parish, Church of the Nativity. We share this simple format with you not only to provide a basic template but also to give you greater insight into what we hope to accomplish in small groups. Feel free to tweak the template as you see fit; just make sure you don't miss the essential principles behind each aspect of an effective small-group meeting.

Before jumping into the format of each meeting, however, allow us to share a few thoughts on the length, the frequency of meetings, and some additional ideas on location. We suggest groups meet somewhere from 75 to 90 minutes. Less than 75 minutes won't be quite enough to get the job done, and for anything longer than 90 minutes, group members will probably not be able to make a regular commitment; it's just too much to ask. We do have groups that fall a little short of those time limits, and some go a little longer (some actually go much longer, which is fine if members have the time to socialize or wish to share a meal together), but most are in that window. The time length will often match the group. A men's group meeting in the morning before work is much more likely to be on the shorter end. A retired couples' group that meets in the evening might choose to linger for dessert and coffee. The exact length will depend on the group affinity.

As for frequency, we encourage groups to meet weekly. At the beginning of our small-group experience at Church of the Nativity, some groups met every other week, but they never lasted. It turns out that just twice a month isn't enough of a commitment to form a habit or achieve cohesion as a group. Of course, inevitably, members will miss meetings for valid reasons, but as we have already noted, their absences have to be carefully monitored.

Our groups meet once a week during the school year, roughly from Labor Day to Father's Day. Many, if not most, groups take a break for the summer (others do not but are responsible for finding their own content). Groups also frequently pause for the holidays and Holy Week.

As we mentioned in the previous chapter, small groups may start at the parish, but they do not meet there long term. Small groups meet in homes, at people's workplaces, at coffee shops, and digitally online.

So now let us break down the small-group format.

1. Gathering Time (10 to 15 Minutes)

Gathering time is a period of transition, getting settled into a break from the busyness of life. If groups meet in the morning, members have had to get up and get going, possibly battling traffic along the way. If they meet in the evening, it is time to just take a breath and let go of the cares of the day. Daytime groups find themselves in between things. Whatever the meeting time is, it requires a few minutes for members to reset.

This is also a time for members to connect casually, in which they can talk about anything from sports to the weather to current family and community events. It is also an opportunity for group members to grab a drink or other refreshments. Coffee and tea or cold drinks are recommended in our experience. Many studies show that just having a drink in hand relaxes people and helps them feel as if they belong.

> **Tom:** In morning groups that I have been part of, we ask guys to just bring their own coffee. Once in a while someone might spring for a box of doughnuts or a bag of bagels, and I've been in groups where we each took a turn providing snacks. But whatever custom you adopt, make sure it is mutually agreed on.

Groups will certainly take on a pattern of their own when it comes to snacks, but the basic encouragement to group leaders is to keep refreshments simple, especially if they are new leaders or just considering leading to lessen the perceived burden. Simple snacks lower the bar for hosting in one's home.

2. Gathering Prayer (5 Minutes)

Once everyone has arrived, greeted one another, and grabbed a beverage, it is time to gather in a circle for prayer. Each small-group session begins with prayer. This can take whatever form the leader feels comfortable leading. Some curriculum comes with scripted prayers the leader can use. Or if the leader is comfortable enough, spontaneous prayers can be powerful. And, of course, there are plenty of resources online. Whatever form the prayer takes, it invites God into the conversation.

> **Tom:** In leading my men's group, I usually just jump in and pray to avoid the awkward moment of asking someone else to do it. Typically, I ask God to bless our time together and that it will help make us better husbands, fathers, sons, brothers, and generally better men as a result of our time together. I might also pray about the topic and that we grow in our understanding of God's Word.

> **Father Michael:** A men's small group that I am currently leading meets late on Friday afternoons and has adopted the custom of praying Vespers from the Liturgy of the Hours. This gives everyone a chance to participate without putting anyone on the spot. It has also turned out to be a beautiful introduction to the Office for the guys who were previously unfamiliar with it (which turned out to be everyone).

The point is that we are gathering together as a Christian community in the conviction that Christ is among us.

3. Content/Presentation (10 Minutes)

Next, the group watches a video or reviews the written material that is being covered that week. As we mentioned in an earlier chapter, the presentation serves to get the group focused on the same topic. It gives direction to the conversation we hope members will have.

4. Questions and Discussion (45 to 75 Minutes)

We provide questions crafted to prompt discussion. This is the heart of the meeting, where the group talks through the content. We usually provide three to five questions. We like to start with some softball questions to help members warm up, just getting to know everyone's initial reaction to the content. More experienced groups might want to skip these kinds of questions and head right for the ones that aim to dig deeper into the topic.

However, the point of the group is not to answer all the questions or get through them efficiently. The point and purpose of the questions is to spur conversation that leads to engagement and connection. They are to help everyone open up about where the topic intersects with their lives. Seasoned small-group leaders will know which questions will work for their group, how to reword questions that don't work, and when to interject questions of their own.

As noted, not all the questions need to be answered. But returning to the questions can be a very helpful tool to get a group back on track once it has wandered off topic in a way that is not really helpful for spiritual reflection and growth. The group leader can find a moment to say, "Hey, let's move on the next question."

When it comes to the *quality* of the conversation, however, the questions are vitally important. If choosing content, make sure the questions provided or the questions you form invite conversation. Yes or no questions are *not* helpful (for example, "Do you agree?"). Loaded questions are *not* helpful (for example, "Why is it dumb not to believe in God?").

We like questions that make people open up (for example, "How does this passage make you feel?"). We especially like questions that ask people to place themselves on a scale (for example, "On a scale of 1 to 5, how much is worry an issue for you right now?"). It gives everyone an opportunity to evaluate themselves and then explain where they are. If there is something going on in their lives, this simple approach can encourage them to really open up and tell their story.

When writing your own questions, or choosing questions, make sure they move from thought to action. The last question should encourage the group to think about what they will *do* as a result of the conversation. Not every meeting will have an action step, but they can add weight to the discussion.

As already noted, our small groups track with our weekend homilies, and also as noted, we preach in message series. At the beginning of a series, we like to provide a question that asks, "What do you hope to get out of this series or learn from it?" Then, at the end of a series, we will ask, "What was your greatest insight or action step you will take as a result of this series?" Basically, it's a question of what's different *after* compared to *before*, reinforcing the whole purpose of the exercise, which is life change.

5. Closing Prayer (5 to 10 Minutes)

We begin the formal part of the meeting in prayer, and we end in prayer too. We like to go around the circle, inviting members to pray out loud, sharing what is on their heart. Let members know they are free to pass; they don't have to feel obligated to pray. But they should be encouraged to do so. Many people who grew up Catholic have no background in giving voice to prayer in front of others. Some will be very awkward prayers, but that's okay. The members are growing in learning how to pray.

Praying out loud is certainly a skill, and one that takes some practice. Groups can be a safe place to practice.

> **Tom:** When I pray at the end of a meeting, I try to keep in mind what the group discussed in the session. If someone shared a concern or a struggle, my

prayer petition will be that the member will know God's grace and presence and what he is doing in their circumstances. If there was a common theme to the meeting, such as passing on faith to our kids, dealing with health concerns, or struggling with finances, I pray for wisdom or courage to take the appropriate step. I try to make the prayer a summation of all we discussed so we are giving it all back to God as an offering and so we can place our trust in him.

So, that's it; it's that simple. There is nothing at all complex, and that's the point. Whether you use our template or something else, keep it simple. This will set small-group leaders up for success and create a consistency for other group members that they can depend on (which will encourage people to keep coming back).

Whatever the format, the aim should be to take the group members on a journey. Groups begin with members having an opportunity to relax and just step back from the stress of the day and the cares of the world. Then, through prayer and focused content, they dive into discussion, helping them to connect the dots between their faith and the responsibilities of life. There is time to learn from one another and to process together and then sum it all up in prayer as an offering to God. That is the journey of each small-group gathering.

FOR REFLECTION AND CONVERSATION

1. Have you experienced small groups previously? How did the format differ from our approach?

2. What aspects of the format will work well in your parish community?

3. How has this chapter helped you better understand the purpose of a group?

| 15 |

Marketing to Members

Marketing is really just about sharing your passion.

—Michael Hyatt

This chapter is intended to help you avoid a mistake (one of many) we made early on with small groups at Church of the Nativity, and the subsequent frustration we faced. Here was our mistake: we thought once we got people into small groups, we'd hit the finish line. After they experienced group life, they would love it so much that they would commit to engaging in Christian community until Jesus comes again. Instead, we found ourselves typically experiencing a large rate of attrition after every change in season or semester. Members would try small groups for Lent, for instance, and then drop off. The attrition felt even more frustrating because people would tell us they had a great experience. Most of the time, parishioners who dropped out didn't do so because they disliked it or even because they failed to see the value of it; they just decided they didn't want to continue.

To grow your small-group program and build the culture appropriate to a parish of small groups, you won't be able to stop at just getting people into groups. You'll need to find ways to retain them.

Tom: At the same time we were struggling to understand the situation with our small-group attrition, I read an article on car advertising and marketing. I had just bought our first minivan for my growing family (one of many minivans we would purchase) and so was inherently interested in the topic. The article noted that car companies, which are among the top spenders in advertising, advertise not just to potential customers but also to recent buyers so they will feel good about making such a significant purchase. The advertising helps them overcome their buyer's remorse, identify with the brand, feel good about their decision, and be motivated to encourage others to buy the same car.

Like car companies, we need to keep advertising and marketing small groups to people who have already bought into joining a group. We must keep affirming their decision until they come to see small groups as a lifestyle choice to which they have firmly committed.

Our role as church leaders is to help people see engaging in small groups as something they do that is core to their identity. We help them to understand that they commit to joining a group not only because of their identity in Christ but also out of a desire to be good husbands and fathers, good wives and mothers, good employers and employees, and all the other things that they are.

If you think about it, Jesus employed this model of motivation in the Sermon on the Mount. Before he explains how his followers should live and behave, he preaches, "You are the salt of the earth. But if salt loses its taste, with what can it be seasoned? It is no longer good for anything but to be thrown out and trampled underfoot. You are the light of the world. A city set on a mountain cannot be hidden" (Mt 5:13–14).

Create communication that not only reinforces the benefits of groups but also appeals to people's identity. Guys who are looking to be great husbands and dads find support in groups. Moms who want to be the best moms ever get to know other moms like them in groups. The following are some suggestions on how you can market groups to your members.

1. The Weekend Homily

We like to say the weekend homily is the "rudder" of the parish "ship." It determines the direction the parish is going in. Therefore, the homily is always the most effective way to communicate the importance of groups. It doesn't have to be a major part of every weekend message. Instead, it can become a go-to aside or often-used illustration. In his homily, making a point about our need for relationships, the preacher can remark, "And that's why we want you in a small group." Or to introduce a story he can say, "I was talking to a guy in my small group . . ." Dropping experiences with small groups into the homily makes groups feel like a normal part of parish life, which is, after all, the goal.

2. Pulpit Announcements

From time to time, you can also use your announcements to remind people about groups. Instead of just announcing events and upcoming activities, talk about small groups. Acknowledge them, thank them, celebrate them.

3. Weekly Emails

Communicate to group members through a weekly email. Create a simple template that includes scripture and scriptural reflection, content comments, "wins," and group member news (births, deaths, weddings, graduations).

4. Social Media

Use your social media accounts to market to your groups. Again, your target is the people already in groups. Post photos of small-group meetings in which people look enthusiastic and engaged. As with the email communication, you can share quotes of small-group members' positive experiences and helpful insights.

5. Group Leaders

Group leaders themselves can also help promote the long-term commitment to stay with these groups. This can best happen through the one-on-one relationships they form with group members. Fellowship that leads to friendship will go a long way to ensure ongoing and long-term commitment.

Those are a few suggestions for continuing to market groups *to your group members.* You may have other ideas. The point is to keep communicating your passion and excitement about groups to the people who choose to give them a shot. Remember, just because someone took a step of experiencing small-group life, it doesn't mean they are fully invested. They may even have buyer's remorse. Keep communicating to new small-group members, and eventually they will experience an identity shift so that they see small groups as a part of their lifestyle.

FOR REFLECTION AND CONVERSATION

1. Identify specific weekends when you will include small groups in your parish-wide communication. Talk to the pastor and ask him to look for ways to drop groups into his homilies

from time to time. Choose a weekend to give a quick update on groups in the announcements.

2. Talk to whoever manages your parish's social media accounts about leveraging them for small groups.

3. Let your small-group leaders know that you would like them to keep raising the question of continuing or ongoing commitment to the groups.

| 16 |

Training and Supporting Ongoing Development of Leaders

The growth and development of people
is the highest calling of leadership.

—Harvey S. Firestone

Tom: Have I mentioned yet that I am from Philly and, as a consequence, a big Eagles fan? Howie Roseman currently serves as the general manager of the team. At least for now, he is considered one of the best in the business. Not long ago I was reading an interview with Roseman about how the team drafted players, and he said something that definitely caught my attention. He said that no player they draft is ready to play in the NFL. They all need to be developed into NFL players. That is astounding. These guys are signed to large contracts, have piles of money invested in them, and played high-stakes football in college, but they still actually need to be developed to play in the NFL.

My point, of course, is not just to talk football, although I appreciate any opportunity to do so! My point is that we need to bring the same perspective to our small-group leaders.

We tend to just plug volunteers into a group as leaders and hope for the best. Part of a plan for any successful small-group ministry will include how to not just train our group leaders but also *develop* them. What's the difference? *Training* means we impart skills to people to undertake the operational aspects of their role. Initial training includes the basics of how to form and run a group.

Developing people means we help leaders grow as individuals and ultimately as Christ followers. Development goes beyond training to consider the whole person. We hope that the experiences they face and challenges they'll handle as group leaders will help them to lean more into Christ and depend upon him to help them lead well.

Both training and development are needed. And we'll honestly admit, we still struggle with this as we continue to learn how to provide both. Training is easier, or at least more obvious; development is harder. The two are not mutually exclusive. Developing leaders just takes training a step further.

Leaders will be most open to training and developing in the first two years of serving. When people are new to leading groups, they can feel intimidated and nervous and, as a result, they will look for all the help they can get. Obviously, the longer someone leads a group, the more comfortable and confident they will become and the less likely it will be that they feel the need for training and development. A good way to engage experienced leaders in training and development is to ask them to play a role in helping new leaders.

So, we can agree we need to train and develop our leaders, but the question is *how*? There are several basic ways that we, at Church of the Nativity, train and develop leaders.

The most basic way we learn and grow is through study. We learn by availing ourselves of books, podcasts, and videos. With effort and discipline, we can gain knowledge we did not have before and insights we had not previously considered. So one way to help your small-group leaders grow and develop is by sharing content. Direct them to books and resources on how to lead groups and chair meetings. Send them short video presentations on small-group life. Maybe create your own library or guide to resources. By equipping your leaders with content they can consume on their own, you are encouraging their growth and development.

Beyond that, it's about actually leading, and then reflecting on the experience of leading. Leading in *reality* is always so much more challenging than leading in *theory*. Until you take action and try to lead something, you will never grow as a leader. However, even that is not enough. You need to *reflect* on your experience to grow as a leader. Wisdom does comes not from experience alone but from taking the time to *reflect* on your experience. You need to identify where you succeeded and what went right so you can replicate the win. You also need to know what went wrong and why it went wrong so you can make the necessary corrections. Reflection helps leaders work smarter and not harder. Actively encourage group leaders to reflect on their experience. Prompt them with emails or texts, providing them with questions for their reflection.

But an important part of any process is always going to be about bringing leaders together. We hope that by creating the right environment and setting up the most helpful conversations, our group leaders strengthen each other. Together they can grow precisely by reflecting upon their experience leading a group. Give them opportunities to celebrate wins, frankly acknowledge challenges, and share best practices.

For newer group leaders, you can do this on a monthly or bimonthly basis. For more experienced group leaders, you will probably only need to bring them together a couple of times a year. Coaching can be part of the process too (see chapter 6). Finally, developing leaders is always about modeling. From the time we are children, we watch other people do something and then we imitate them. As your ministry gains momentum and more and more members experience small-group life, they will learn in this manner. After enjoying a small-group experience for a season or two, they will be more likely to step up and serve as group leaders. And having had a positive experience, it will be all the easier to train and develop them. Of course, the question remains, what exactly are we training and developing leaders in or to do?

1. Learning Group Dynamics

We are helping group leaders to grow in dealing with conflict among members, how to handle problem people in the group (see chapter 18), and generally help build a group culture of civility and mutual respect.

2. Advancing in Personal Faith

Effectively facilitating a faith-based small group is more than a skill to be learned, it is a gift of the Holy Spirit. In fact, it calls upon all the gifts of the Holy Spirit: wisdom, understanding, counsel, fortitude, knowledge, piety, and fear of the Lord.

The gifts of the Spirit, given in Baptism and sealed in Confirmation, are nurtured in the virtuous path of discipleship. We want to invest in our group leaders and help *them* grow as disciples of Jesus Christ. We especially want to help them connect the dots on how serving as a group leader is a way they grow as a Christ

follower, because growing disciples are going to be more successful at growing disciples.

3. Growing in Prayer

Above all, advancing in faith means growing in prayer. Prayer is
an essential part of group life, and so we want to help our leaders
improve the quality and depth of prayer in their groups and in
their personal spirituality. When you bring group leaders together,
they should share resources and discuss best practices they're
finding for making prayer a priority and a powerful aspect of
their groups.

4. Establishing Boundaries

Leaders will also need to establish boundaries, especially when
it comes to providing care in the ways we identify in the next
paragraphs. Neediness, in its many forms and faces, will almost
certainly present itself in any group experience. Financial needs,
health concerns and crises, marital disputes and difficulties, loss,
grief, and the list goes on and on.

We want to help leaders understand the limits of groups.
Group members can offer care by providing meals on difficult
days, serving as a listening ear, or simply praying for and encouraging one another through difficult times. Attending funerals or
wake services when a group member loses a loved one and check-
ing in on prayer requests are all certainly appropriate and will be
appreciated. We want to help our leaders understand those opportunities and help their group meet those needs.

At the same time, groups can lose their effectiveness and be
unhelpful if they start trying to solve every problem, manage every
move, reverse every unfortunate situation. Long-standing marital
issues, various mental health concerns, complicated legal entan-
glements, for example, are beyond the scope of what a small group

can handle. A developing leader will become adept at recognizing the difference, helping the member in need to seek help beyond the group.

> **Father Michael:** I was reminded of this with a new group formed here at the parish a few years ago. The group included a member who was deeply depressed and, in fact, mentally unstable. He repeatedly said things in the group suggesting self-harm. The leaders of the group were new as well. They tried to handle the problem as best they could but failed to manage the situation or make any real impact. That failure, in turn, loomed large over each gathering of the group. Eventually, they came to me and together, in a loving and gracious way, we helped the guy step out of the group and into the professional help he needed.

As we mentioned earlier, small-group leaders are essential to keeping our small groups strong and moving them in the same direction. Since vision can diminish and people tend to forget why we do what we do, it will be important to remind leaders that small groups are about spiritual growth and relationships.

FOR REFLECTION AND CONVERSATION

1. In what ways have you developed as a leader? What have been the most helpful and impactful ways?

2. How often do you want to bring your small-group leaders together? Take a look at the calendar and set aside some dates for the year ahead.

3. Of the four areas of training and development addressed in the list above, which do you think is most important right now for your leaders and small-group ministry? Is there anything you would add or subtract from the list?

STEP VII

Persevere

| 17 |

Naming Common Small-Group Problems

Every problem has in it the seeds of its own solution.

—Norman Vincent Peale

Someone once said, "Ministry would be easy if it wasn't for the people." We've said it and continue to say it often. Building a small-group ministry will solve many problems for your parish, help build fellowship, and produce much other good fruit. But it will create problems too. You will especially encounter difficulties in the beginning as you learn to help group leaders address the operational and interpersonal challenges in their groups.

Our role as parish leaders is not to solve all the problems ourselves but to empathize with our group leaders and eventually equip them to resolve or at least address and clarify problems. This is all part of discipleship growth. God uses the disappointing behavior and rough edges people present to build our character and improve our emotional health.

In this chapter we present a few of the most common problems that small-group leaders will face in their groups. Before you get into them, refer back to chapter 10 and the values we have found helpful. Creating a contract, spoken or written, that enumerates values governing the group will be incredibly helpful in dealing with small-group problems. The contract will give you a foundation or base line of expectations for your small-group leaders to use when addressing the problems they encounter. The group values will serve as conversation starters so that any tensions that develop are seen in a more objective way and not taken personally, or at least a little less personally.

1. Irregular Attendance

In building a small-group ministry, attendance will probably be the number one frustration for group leaders (as explained in chapter 10). To help them deal with the issue, dig into the details. How many *are* showing up and *who*? Are the same people attending each week? Maybe that core group is the real group. Recognize that is a win in itself and should be celebrated. Are the same people not showing up each week? They need to be challenged to choose if they want to be in the group or respectfully step back.

On the other hand, perhaps there are no patterns; it's just poor attendance week after week, and really, everyone is guilty. Then it's time for a frank discussion about the real reasons for such apathy. The problem might be fixable, such as finding a new time or place. Perhaps the problem is only temporary because of the multiplication of commitments in a busy time of year, and the group needs to press pause. Sometimes the problem is unfixable, maybe a bad mix of personalities, and the group needs to dissolve. This sometimes happens, and really, no one is to blame.

The one thing that you don't want to do is ignore the problem. That would be disrespectful to those who make the effort to attend, as well as disrespectful to other groups. Irregular attendance inherently sends the message that this really isn't that important.

If a group leader just cannot, for whatever reason, get people to come to their group, there might be a problem with the leader. Perhaps he or she doesn't have the skills to lead a group, or for some other reason the person just isn't the right fit for leadership of this group at this time. If you are not sure you would want to be in a group led by that leader, pay attention to that instinct. Suggest the leader join a group for a season and learn how to lead from that other group leader.

2. Bad Theology

In our groups we are going to have members who don't adhere to all of the teachings and disciplines of the Church or even believe the basic doctrines of Christianity. For some others, it might be because they are uneducated in their Catholic faith. Perhaps they are new to the Church, and it's still all unclear to them. Maybe they are actually misinformed about what we believe. Still others simply have thoughtful and carefully considered beliefs and convictions at odds with Catholicism. So, how do we equip our small-group leaders to deal with bad theology or views clearly contradictory with our Catholic faith?

Before answering directly, we remind group leaders that the point of small groups is all about relationships and growing in faith through "life-on-life" interaction. The primary focus for groups is building relationships and not teaching doctrine or studying theology. So, their first role is to preserve an environment that emphasizes and honors relationships and ensures people can speak freely. We are not saying that doctrine can be dismissed and truth doesn't matter. Nor do we want our groups to be stirring up confusion about what the Church teaches. The right ideas about God are vitally important to growing in faith, but *how* we lead people to those ideas in a small group looks much different than in a classroom. So, any challenge to the person must be done in the context of a loving and mutually respectful relationship.

Begin addressing the problem by seeking to understand the other's point of view and exactly how they came to it. The conversation, which might best be a sidebar, away from the whole group, should be conducted in charity. Also, encourage group leaders to challenge members to think through what is being expressed. Is it really *bad* theology or just a point of disagreement? Invite leaders to make this assessment, which we learned from others:

Is it *acceptable* for people of faith to disagree on *this* particular issue, still worship together in the same parish, and enjoy fellowship in the same small group? If so, then there is nothing to address; clarify the Tradition or teaching of the Church and agree to disagree.

Is it *unacceptable* to disagree on this issue and remain in communion? The group can discuss why they hold different opinions, perhaps bringing in a mediator to facilitate the conversation. Certainly, the moment should be used as a teaching moment for everyone to grow in understanding our Catholic faith. It is possible that in some cases the group will need to disband.

> **Tom:** Sometimes bad theology can just come out of nowhere. In one of my groups, a member was suddenly describing the "swoon theory" that Jesus didn't really die on the Cross. Instead, he was still alive when he was taken off the Cross and placed in the tomb. Subsequently he then went off to Egypt to preach and teach. As the guy described this theory, he became increasingly animated, as if he might be sharing some new insight with the group. I responded very gently, "Yes, that is an old argument against the Resurrection that many people have held. It was why John writes in his gospel that a soldier pierced Jesus's side and blood and water flowed out, John's point being that in that

moment Jesus was clearly, unarguably dead." That was my attempt to right the wrong and redirect the conversation while respecting the guy himself. We then moved on to another question, and he was not offended.

The general guidance for group leaders is to let them know not to be afraid if someone expresses an opinion that stands in contrast with Catholic teaching or core Christian doctrine. Even if a conversation picks up steam, even if it is going off the rails, they can press pause and speak up for the Church. Leaders can always say something along the lines of "That's not my under-standing of Church teaching or Christian doctrine. Let me do some research, get feedback from the parish on that issue, and bring it back next week." Or better yet, if there is a member solid in their faith, encourage them to do some research and report back to the group.

3. Acceptance of Sin or a Sinful Lifestyle

If our groups are working well, members will honestly acknowl-edge their faults and failures. That is very helpful and healthy. If the purpose is conversations that lead to conversion, then mem-bers will share their struggles with sin and their progress toward the goal of life change. In those moments, a healthy group will simply give grace and acceptance to a member. However, some-times a member of a group or even the whole group needs to be challenged. Being attentive and respectful is to be encouraged, accepting unvirtuous attitudes should not be.

> **Father Michael:** I remember being in an otherwise supportive and helpful group that, one evening, took a very dark turn. One member described in

detail the devolution of his relationship with his siblings and his determination to have nothing more to do with them. This fueled others to pile on with their own sad stories of sibling rivalry and conflicts with the ensuing lack of reconciliation and dismissive attitudes toward the idea of forgiveness. The conversation unfolded so quickly and the emotions ran so deep, I hardly knew what to say, so I said nothing. The evening ended on a distinctly unchristian note, entirely unmindful of Jesus's clear teaching to forgive and forgive often (Mt 18).

During the intervening week, I prayed about what I would say to the group without coming across as insensitive toward the pain they had obviously experienced in their relationships. As our group discussion got started, I asked for a few minutes to retrace our steps back to the previous discussion. Gently laying out the Lord's mandate to forgive from the heart, as given ultimate expression from the Cross, I invited them to look into their own hearts. If reconciliation was simply not possible, or even a good idea, forgiveness was always still possible and necessary. We ended up having a really great conversation that evening.

Besides sinful *attitudes*, leaders might run into the acceptance of sinful *lifestyles*. When someone confesses a sin and asks for prayers to change, we certainly want them to know they have our support. We all sin and fall short of the glory of God. Healthy and growing groups will acknowledge that and encourage one another to receive God's mercy and to overcome sin by his grace.

When someone acknowledges a sin, that is one thing. It is another thing entirely when there is a presumed or tacit approval of sin. This might be one of the most uncomfortable problems group leaders face. Just like the issue with bad theology, there are some questions to ask first. Is it sin or just a point of disagreement or difference in perception? If the latter, then it isn't anything to address.

Other questions to consider are how long has the group been meeting, what is the depth of the relationship, and what is the spiritual maturity of the member? Acceptance paves the way to influence. So, in a new group or with a new group member, it is important that relationships are given time to form and grow strong so that acceptance is felt. It is also important that someone trying a group out as their first spiritual step doesn't feel attacked or rejected. If someone on the fringes of faith tries a group out for the first time, then you don't want to scare him or her off by challenging them right away. But once there is depth of relationship and trust in the bank account, it is time to offer the appropriate challenge.

> **Tom:** A member of my small group went through a terrible divorce. I knew his story and knew well he had done everything he could to save the marriage, but his ex-wife wanted no part in it. A few years later he started dating someone, and eventually it became clear they were living together. This remained unaddressed in group discussion, giving tacit approval to the arrangement. That bothered me, especially since the guy had teenage sons to whom he should have been giving a better example.

After one of our group meetings, I pulled him aside. Asking for permission to challenge him, I brought up the situation. I didn't have to say much before he knew where I was going. He appreciated the challenge and took it to heart, opening the door to conversation in the group. He shared his reluctance to marry again given his previous experience, even though he knew in his heart he had found the right person. Everyone offered support, and one of the guys provided really helpful encouragement, describing his own journey from divorce through the annulment process to remarriage. Long story short, he eventually did remarry and the group celebrated with him.

A fourth problem requires much more discussion and exploration. In the next chapter we will look at how to deal with the personalities that can disrupt a small group.

FOR REFLECTION AND CONVERSATION

1. Which of these issues do you think would be most difficult for group leaders to address effectively?

2. Did you find yourself agreeing with the advice for group leaders? Why or why not?

3. What different advice would you offer group leaders? What additional advice would you add?

| 18 |

Dealing with "EGR" People

People are not problems to be solved.
They are mysteries to be explored.

—Pastor Eugene H. Peterson

In the last chapter we looked at three common problems you will find in your small-group ministry. In this chapter we will dive into just one that will come in various forms: dealing with EGR people. What is an EGR person? Simply put, it is someone who comes with *extra grace required* (EGR).

It is the group member who is a little like sandpaper—they are a bit irritating and can rub the group the wrong way. Every group has one, and if you don't know who it is . . . then it is probably you. There are a variety of *extra grace required* people, so just defining their unhelpful behavior can be very helpful. Sometimes group leaders will know something isn't quite right but can't define it. We hope the following list proves useful in helping leaders put their finger on the problem, making it easier to address. Some of this material is informed by Bill Willits's excellent book on small groups, *Creating Community*.

The Non-Talker

This is the member who does not say anything, at all, ever! In some ways it is a small issue compared to the other issues we'll discuss.

The main difficulty with the non-talker is that they leave everyone else wondering what they're thinking, or if they've checked out entirely. This in turn creates awkwardness in the group.

Sometimes those who speak the least actually have the most to contribute. Perhaps, it just takes them a while to warm up and get comfortable with the group. With support and encouragement they can change over time. The way to deal with a non-talker is to ask him or her direct questions from time to time and give space for the response.

The Dominator

On the other end of the spectrum is the member who cannot be quiet, who talks and talks and talks. This can take various forms. Sometimes the person can get preachy and start telling other people how to live their lives or what to think on a given issue. Sometimes, the dominator acts as if they are the teacher and the group is his or her class. Dominators are just natural talkers and external processors who easily go on tangent after tangent; maybe they don't know they are doing it. Usually, they just need to be made aware of how much they are dominating the group. Let them know you want to give everyone a chance to speak, as a way to show respect to other members of the group.

> **Tom:** In one of my small groups, I had a guy I really liked a lot, but he drove me crazy because he would go on and on about everything and go off on just about anything. I'd like to say I addressed it, but I didn't. Thankfully, I had a great co-leader, Dave. Dave knew I was frustrated, so he took the member aside and asked him to promise to be a little more self-aware. They even agreed on a discreet signal Dave would give him if he was talking too

much. The member received this challenge with grace, and I could see the difference at the very next meeting. This new skill most definitely helped him in his other relationships at home and at work.

The Interrupter

This is the member who will cut others off and burst into the conversation. Often, but not necessarily, they can also be a dominator. They shoot others down, effectively shutting them up because they have to make their point or argue their position. As you would with the dominator, make the interrupter aware of his or her tendency to interrupt others. Remind the interrupter of the value of respect for other group members, and that means giving everyone a chance to fully express their thoughts. Make respectful listening a core commitment of group discussion.

The One-Upper

This is the person who has to share their problems, struggles, and experiences whenever someone else does. In their minds, their problems, struggles, and experiences are always more pressing, more consequential, and of more relevance to the group than everyone else's—just as in poker when someone raises the stakes: "I'll see your problem child and raise you with my even bigger problem child." It diminishes the other members of the group and communicates that they don't really matter. If the one-upper does it even once they'll do it again, so gently take an early opportunity to let them know about the pattern they are demonstrating and to be aware of the impact it has on others. Here again, respectful listening needs to be addressed by the leader.

The Know-It-All

Closely related to the one-upper is the know-it-all. Perhaps he or she has some seminary experience, or a theological or biblical background, maybe they've worked in a church previously. Whatever the backstory, they just know more about many of the topics under discussion than anyone else. And as a result, they find themselves supplying information as a regular feature of group meetings. Although not entirely a bad thing, it can have a stultifying effect on the group and make people feel unqualified to join in. This situation will require some adeptness and perhaps even humor to keep the conversation going and consistently include everyone.

The Fixer

This is the individual who gives advice to everyone about everything. Whatever problem you have, they have the solution, whatever question you're facing, they know the answer, even if they don't. In our groups we want shared wisdom from experience, we don't want members trying to "fix" one another, especially if they have never experienced the problem in question. Let the fixer know that sometimes people have to come to a resolution on their own and that the group is not always there to find a solution for them.

If they actually do have some experience with a problem another member is having, encourage him or her to ask permission before offering advice. Invite them to say, "I have had a similar struggle, do you mind if I give you some advice or thoughts on how to handle the problem?" Just encouraging him or her to ask the question first might slow down their propensity to give unsolicited advice.

The Lacerator

Rare, but not unknown, this member cuts down other members, especially absent ones, through biting observations or sarcastic comments. While other problems can be overlooked from time to time or even tolerated for a time, this behavior needs to be addressed immediately. A group will be damaged, eventually diminished, and even divided, becoming a toxic environment on the way to division. The issue needs to be dealt with lovingly yet firmly. Have a one-on-one conversation to address the issue. If it continues, the person may need to be asked to leave the group.

The Repeater

This is the person who repeats themselves and sounds like a broken record, bringing up the same issue time after time, week after week. Often it is because they have a major problem in their life that needs to be addressed beyond the group, probably in a professional setting. Find a discreet, respectful way to let this member know that while the group is there to support him or her, it is not a support group. They might need some additional help. Walk with them as they seek the help they need.

The Pretend Listener

This is a common problem in many groups. One or more members aren't really listening when others are speaking. They are patiently (or *not* so patiently) waiting for their turn to talk. And the pretend listener always gives themselves away because what they have to say has nothing to do with what the previous speaker was discussing. The response to the pretend listener is simple: the group leader needs to step in and return the conversation to the previous topic: "Thanks, John, but can we return for a moment to what Joe was discussing?"

> **Tom:** My worst tendency would be as an "inter-
> rupter." If I get excited and want to make a point, I
> can find myself cutting others off or trying to talk
> over them. Especially when something sparks my
> interest or touches on strong convictions, I can
> become loud.

> **Father Michael:** I tend to be the "fixer" in my
> group, and being the pastor only aggravates that
> tendency. Whenever an issue or problem comes
> up, everyone turns to me for the "right" answer.
> And more often than not, without stopping to con-
> sider what I'm doing, I just jump in and provide
> the answer.

In each of these categories, the person is putting the spotlight on
themselves. But groups are meant to be an exchange of grace and
truth in which we move from independence to interdependence.

Many of these challenging scenarios in groups are best handled outside the group, one-on-one. In helping small-group leaders
discern whether to address the issues or not, ask if it is an occasional problem or habitual. If occasional, then maybe it is something to let go. If habitual, and hurting the health of the group,
then it needs to be addressed. However, a very useful exercise for
the group might be to begin their time together reviewing each of
these negative behaviors, with each member asked to self-identify
their own tendencies. This might even be a worthwhile exercise
on a semiannual basis. If the group does this exercise, then the
small-group leader should go first.

Of course, these challenges require discernment and prayer.
We can encourage group leaders in these practices so that they
grow through these challenges as leaders and as disciples of Jesus
Christ. Keep in mind that beyond the good of the group, God

may well be calling the group leader to have the difficult conversation with the member for the sake of the member's own good and growth. If someone demonstrates unhelpful behaviors in the group, they might very well be (and probably are) acting in exactly the same way in the workplace, at home, and in other relationships too. Small groups can be excellent environments to learn new, more helpful behaviors.

FOR REFLECTION AND CONVERSATION

1. Which of these negative tendencies are you most likely to fall into?

2. Have you found any additional types of personalities that disrupt a group? If so, name them and describe them.

3. Do you agree with the methods given when working with *extra grace required* people? What other ways would you counsel small-group leaders to handle EGR people?

| 19 |

Forming an Annual Plan

The man who is prepared has his battle half fought.
—Miguel de Cervantes

It's been said that if you fail to plan then you plan to fail. Some people (Father Michael) like to plan and some people (Tom) don't, but if you want to see small groups succeed in the long haul at your parish, then it is essential you put together an annual plan for groups.

Planning brings frustration for planners and non-planners alike. It's frustrating for non-planners because it forces them to slow down and look to the future instead of just forging ahead at full speed with whatever is next. It's frustrating for planners because nothing ever *goes* as planned.

But it must be done.

One of the greatest plans ever executed was the D-Day invasion of World War II under the command of Dwight D. Eisenhower, who famously said, "Before the battle plans are everything, during the battle plans are nothing." Plans can help you prepare for battle, but you have to hold them loosely and stay adaptable.

Another World War II general, George Patton, offered another insight: "An imperfect plan executed today is better than a perfect plan executed tomorrow." Plans are needed and necessary, but don't spend so much time making plans that you don't get around to executing them. An effective annual plan will include four key elements.

1. "Smart" Goal Setting

You will want to put together a list of goals for your group program in the year ahead that are "SMART" goals: specific, measurable, achievable, realistic (yet a bit risky), and time sensitive. And, of course, there are many different types of goals you may want to set.

One goal might center on growth, which means just getting more people into small groups. Now that you have launched your ministry, your goal might be to grow groups by 20 or 30 percent. Or maybe you will set a goal for the overall number of people you hope will get into a group. As we've mentioned, a few years ago we set a crazy goal of getting a thousand new people into a group (just for Lent). We knew not everyone would stay in their groups beyond Lent, but we wanted everyone to at least experience groups. Yes, we did make our goal, and yes, many left their groups after Lent. During the last few years, we have been setting a big goal of growing groups every *other* year so that we experience a growth spurt and then consolidate our growth.

Another goal might be focused on training and developing your small-group leaders and coaches. The first growth is about growing *wider* by involving more people in groups. This type of growth will be about going *deeper* and making your small groups more effective by making your leadership more effective and stronger.

Focusing on improving the retention of current group members could be an excellent goal to improve your ministry. Maybe you have launched groups and succeeded in getting people on board, but for whatever reason people have not stayed with them. This is actually a common and consistent problem with groups everywhere. You may set a goal to collect accurate data on what exactly your retention rate is and *why* people don't stick with groups, and then set a goal to retain more people.

Perhaps reaching out to a certain demographic, underrepresented among current group members, could be a really challenging and rewarding goal. For example, two groups we have struggled to reach at Church of the Nativity are dads with young children and college students. Over the last few years, we have very deliberately put effort into reaching both groups. Last year, our director of small groups, Susan, brought together dads who were already committed to groups to help us with their cohort. As a result of this effort, we've launched two dozen new dads' groups this past year. More recently, we have rewritten the job description of a young staffer, Leah, so that she directs about half of her time investing in young adults. This extra effort and energy have already been fruitful as more and more young adults engage in group life and the life of the parish.

Another goal might be to improve the operational side of small groups. Maybe you want to work on making it easier for people to sign up or clean up your database or develop ways to communicate with groups. These goals often go together.

You may set a goal of getting group members serving together in the wider community in various service projects sponsored by the parish. Promoting Eucharistic Adoration, regular Confession, or attendance at daily Mass among group members are also great goals.

We hope this gives you some ideas about the kinds of goals you might want to set for groups at your parish. Or maybe they've sparked some other thoughts. Whatever goals you set should be aimed at helping you drive small groups to grow deeper and wider. Remember, growing wider means helping more people into group life. Growing deeper means helping groups become more effective at making disciples.

2. Calendaring

Once you set your goals, you will want to plan your calendar in light of those goals. Along with scheduling events and meetings that support your specific goals, you will want to make sure you schedule some of the following.

Launch Weekends

Even if you set modest growth goals for groups, you will want to set aside one or two weekends during the year when you remind the parish of the value of small groups and invite them to join one. By scheduling these weekends, you will plant a small-group culture deeper into the life of the parish, encouraging more parishioners to get on board.

Data Cleanup

Two to three times a year you will want to schedule a specific time when you reach out to leaders and ask them to identify their group members and provide their contact information. Groups are an ever-changing reality, with members constantly coming and going, so keeping accurate data is an ongoing task. This information will allow you to know which groups can welcome new members as you prepare your next launch.

Training and Investment in Group Leaders

Set dates to bring your small-group leaders together for training and development. The training for leaders could be in person or online. You may want to schedule a new leader welcome event in the fall or a celebration event in the spring to thank group leaders for their investment in groups. Consider doing a mini-retreat at another time in the year to encourage group leaders and cast a vision for the future. There are many ways you can invest in and thank your leaders. Feel free to be creative; just make sure you schedule it so all participants can plan to attend.

Communications Schedule

Map out a plan for a communications schedule for your group leaders, members, and parishioners. In your plan, determine how often you will reach out to each of your audiences. Pay special attention to your small-group leaders. You will want to communicate with them more consistently than the other groups. Plan to communicate with your group leaders at least once a month or even more frequently. During the school year, our small-group leaders receive a weekly newsletter with information on the current small-group content and events in the parish.

Evaluation

Identify a time when you will *evaluate* your leaders and coaches. Create a simple evaluation form asking the team how they are enjoying their volunteer ministry. In church world, we tend to put people into ministry roles so that we are filling open positions, with little consideration for how well a fit it is. If serving is no longer helping an individual grow closer to Christ, then we move them on to other service in the parish. On the other hand, if the year has gone well, we want to celebrate the good things God is doing in their lives and through their leadership.

Meeting Schedule

It will be helpful for you to put together a suggested schedule for group meetings. As we mentioned earlier, we encourage groups to meet on a weekly basis, ideally from Labor Day through Father's Day. It just makes sense for groups to take breaks at Christmas, during Holy Week, and over the summer. Taking some time to lay out this suggested calendar for groups will help them get on the same page.

3. Content Planning

We've already discussed content (see chapter 9), explaining how we connect our content plan to our weekend message (homily) series. In late April/early May certain staff members and interested parishioners get together and plan out the year. We break down our fall season into three different series: kickoff, late fall, and Advent. The Advent series is four weeks in length; the other two series are five or six weeks. Fall is always a sprint to Christmas and the more you can use the summer to plan it all out, the stronger the season will be. We always do a New Year's series, a Lenten series, and an Easter series. Each of those series runs five or six weeks.

As we have already—perhaps painstakingly—emphasized, our recommendation is to offer small groups in tandem with your weekend preaching. If you plan out your year in message series as a parish, planning your small-group content will be much easier.

4. Budgeting

As has been said, if you want to know what someone values, look at their schedule and look at their budgeting. How we spend our money and how we spend our time reveals what we value. To be a church of small groups, we must invest money in them. The biggest budget item to consider will be staffing. You may not be able to start there, but eventually you will want to invest money in at least a part-time staff member who is on the payroll or a volunteer director who needs to be compensated in some fashion. Either way, this is someone who can champion small groups and drive them forward.

When budgeting, you will also need to consider content. If you purchase content or develop your own, it will require some kind of financial investment. We have created a library of small-group content, which can be found at rebuiltparish.com. For a small yearly fee you can have access to all the small-group videos we have created.

Along with staff and content, you will need to budget for events, marketing, thank-you gifts for your volunteers, and training materials for your group leaders. Events can require food and refreshments. Marketing may mean signage as well as giveaways such as T-shirts. Thanking volunteers will also require some investment: we like to say "volunteers aren't free."

As you can see, there is much to consider in putting together your annual plan. However, don't allow the details to overwhelm you. The point is to put some thought and effort into planning, knowing that it will prepare you for a successful year.

FOR REFLECTION AND CONVERSATION

1. What goals do you want to create for small groups in the year ahead?

2. Set a date to bring your team together for an offsite meeting so you can set and prioritize those goals.

3. Use the list above to put together your annual plan for groups. Decide now when you will complete the plan.

| 20 |

Undertaking a Long Obedience in the Same Direction

Success is not final, failure is not fatal:
It is the courage to continue that counts.

—Winston Churchill

It takes time to establish a clear and consistent culture in which people connect in groups. That's challenging because we always want success right away, as in the first season. It probably won't happen. Building a sustainable small-group program will take perseverance, which is all about a long obedience in the same direction.

Tom: We can guarantee that you will face difficulties, encounter obstacles, and experience discouragement along the way. We know from our own experience. Boy, oh boy, do we know! We started with just two groups; Father Michael led one, and I led the other. We tried to form a leadership team with two women (whom we didn't really know) who came forward expressing interest and support.

One was a support . . . until her sudden and most untimely death. The other, just a couple of weeks into the effort, with absolutely no warning, up and quit—the program *and* the parish. To this day we have no idea why she left or where she went. It was deeply disappointing, but we kept going.

Father Michael: Still not really knowing what we were doing and with just two groups, for our second season we went ahead and added five more. A couple of them were successful enough that we assumed we had arrived at the Promised Land. So, the very next year we did something incredibly bold: We launched groups to the whole parish for Lent, as we've mentioned before. That's right, we launched groups to the *whole* parish. To our credit, we were very successful in getting people into groups since about half the parish responded to our invitation. As previously noted, we attributed that success to a combination of favorable factors. Most of our groups met here on campus, the commitment was solidly just for Lent, and we gave everyone who signed up a free book that formed the basis of our content that season.

Unfortunately, our success was short-lived. Our data collection was woefully inadequate for the numbers we were dealing with. We had trouble identifying and maintaining reliable leaders (all of whom were obviously new leaders). We struggled to help them handle problems and problem people, of which there were plenty in that early effort. Perhaps most of all, having so many groups on campus, at various times of day and different days of the week, proved a logistical nightmare. And, as we've already acknowledged, our rate of retention throughout the season was disappointing, to say the least. When most all the groups disbanded after Easter, we felt we were back to square one. But we persevered.

We share these struggles with you not to discourage you but rather to encourage and inspire you. We hope it helps in two ways.

First, when you hit difficulties, you will know that they are to be expected and it's definitely not *you*. Don't take it personally. You are not a failure for hitting these challenges. You are not doing something wrong; in fact, you are doing something right. When building anything of value, we will have troubles and struggles, we will face opposition. And when undertaking a kingdom-building project such as a small-group ministry, the forces of darkness will oppose us. So don't let that depress or defeat you. Keep going.

Second, we share our struggles to let you know that it is worth it. Despite all the frustrations and failures we encountered, we are glad we invested in small groups. It has been well worth our efforts. We continue to see the fruit of those efforts a decade later. By building a church of small groups, you sow seeds that will reap far more than you can imagine.

Jesus went through the pain of the Passion because he understood the joy that was on the other side of Calvary. By choosing to build a small-group program, you are for sure taking up a cross. To keep going, you must focus on the joy that will come from it. Envision what could be and should be in your parish that does not yet exist. As we read about Jesus in Hebrews 12:2, "For the sake of the joy that lay before him he endured the cross."

Consider concrete images that will motivate you to keep building the program.

You may be motivated by the image that comes to mind of one day hosting a small-group launch, with dozens of small-group leaders excitedly signing up dozens and dozens of parishioners for their first-time group experience. Or your inspiration might come in learning of a couples' group sitting in a circle, praying for one another's marriages and laughing together as they share the joys and struggles of parenthood.

Hearing about small-group members coming through for one another during difficult times might form part of your vision. Imagine one day getting an email from a parishioner thanking you for building a small-group ministry because when they were sick or suffering, their group cared for them. Or maybe you hope to eventually have a conversation with a young dad, who having long neglected his faith, has come back to faith and the Church through his group. The experience turned out to be deeply enriching for his family life too.

We don't know what got you started on this small-group journey or what motivates you moving forward, but it is important to name it. A clear vision of small groups will help you push past the challenges and disappointments so you can co-create a brighter future with the Lord. To help you name that vision, we close with a few testimonies from our parish. These are the types of stories that motivate us to keep inviting people into small groups and help other parishes across the country build small-group ministries. We look forward to the day when you will receive testimonies like these.

My small group has been a positive influence in every aspect of my life: my faith development, my prayer life, and in my marriage. Stepping into a safe space every week to explore my questions about my relationship with God, the Church, and with others, I'm more honest about how I'm feeling and where I want and need to grow.

I joined a small group because I was new to Nativity and just wanted to make some friends. And I did! I have made some lifelong friends. But little did I know that they would become my life line and support system after my husband was diagnosed with cancer. I don't know what I would have done without them.

My life appeared to be great to everyone looking from the outside. I made sure of that! In reality, I was going through a terrible divorce, my business and finances were negatively impacted by COVID, my daughter was struggling with her college experience, and I was escaping all of it and avoiding reality by drinking heavily.

Joining a small group was the very last thing I ever thought that I would do. I only gave it a try at the urging of a friend. What I quickly learned was that I'd had no idea what I had been missing. Frankly, my problems haven't magically gone away, my circumstances haven't really changed in any significant way to outward appearances. But on the inside, I am transformed. I'm hopeful again.

Faith was never a priority for me. It was like an "add-on activity." That is, until I joined my young adult small group. Being in a Catholic community with other college-aged people inspired me. God is now part of my everyday life, and it's because I have my small group to encourage me, hold me accountable, and help me grow in my faith through love of God and others. I have come to realize that God has a plan for me, and I can choose to live in relationship with him and follow that plan.

For twenty years I've been filled with shame over my abortion. I was weighed down with the burden of this secret until coming to my small group and opening myself up to the hope of healing.

After getting to know my small group, I felt safe sharing my secret with them, thereby opening myself to the miraculous healing that God wanted for me. I can now move forward in my life and help others who are experiencing this pain while feeling a new freedom I had come to think I would never know again.

Men don't know how to ask for help; we are not taught how to share our feelings. We're encouraged to hide our feelings, or even deny them. So, as we men move through the seasons of life—and they bring us new challenges—we often find ourselves alone . . . alone to face our problems, alone to carry our problems, alone to solve our problems.

Self-doubt, shortcomings, and sin are also isolating. Assuming that I alone am falling short of perfection leaves me feeling very much more alone. Even in an age in which technology provides access to the world, and connection to people everywhere, living in a community where casual friendships are easy to make, there was an inescapable aloneness to my life. My small-group experience, not at once but little by little, filled that void. I discovered others who cared with me as I struggled with illness, dealt with troubled teens, transitioned jobs, and mourned the passing of family members. They also shared with me many joys: births, graduations, marriages, a new job! It helps to share our burdens, but we must have someone with whom to share our joys.

I know now that I am my brother's keeper.

Nobody should be alone. And together in Christ, we never have to be.

| Appendix A |

Frequently Asked Questions about Small Groups

What is a small group?

A small group is a group of six to ten people who gather on a regular (preferably weekly) basis to pray, discuss their faith (focused on specific topics), and connect together in fellowship.

What is the purpose of small groups?

The purpose of small groups is to help parishioners identify friends in faith. They are primarily about connecting members of the parish in order to learn from one another's faith.

What do you do in small groups?

At our parish, Church of the Nativity, we follow a simple format. We gather informally for ten to fifteen minutes. Then we begin with prayer. We watch a video presentation or listen to a specific reading from the weekend liturgy. Next, we turn to discussion questions and finally end in prayer. It's simple but effective: good things happen when bringing people together who want to grow in their faith.

Where do groups meet?

Groups meet in homes, offices, local coffee shops, and online. It all depends on the group. Under certain conditions, groups meet at church.

How long is a group meeting?

Most group meetings are about 75 to 90 minutes.

What's my commitment to a group?

It's up to you, a single season (like Lent or Advent) could be a place to start. Ultimately, our goal at Nativity is for people to make an ongoing commitment to small groups a lifestyle choice.

| Appendix B |

Answering Six Common Objections to Small Groups

Below are some common objections to small groups that you might face (we did). Our hope is that you can easily overcome these objections that keep people from joining groups and perhaps keep you from even trying.

1. Small groups are just a Protestant thing.

Actually, if you recognize that Church history reaches back to the age of the apostles, then groups are very much a Catholic thing. Acts of the Apostles tells us that the first Christian communities met in the Temple courts and in homes (Acts 5:42). We can bookend that ancient text with St. John Paul, who wrote,

> So that all parishes . . . may be truly communities of Christians, local ecclesial authorities ought to foster . . . small, basic or so-called "living" communities, where the faithful can communicate the Word of God and express it in service and love to one another; these communities are true expressions of ecclesial communion and centers of evangelization, in communion with their pastors. (John Paul II, *Christifideles Laici* [*On the Vocation and the Mission of the Lay Faithful in the Church and in the World*], 26)

2. Small groups will create gossip circles or unhealthy cliques.

We admit they have the potential to do so, if they are not given proper direction and clear guidelines. With well-trained leadership, small groups can be environments that foster spiritual growth, connect members of the parish to one another, and lead group members to greater engagement in the life of the parish. With the right mix of planning, training, and ongoing support, groups can actually discourage gossip and in their openness prevent cliques.

3. Small groups will stir up problems that people already have, making them worse.

This can be true on occasion, but it is not a strong argument against small groups. Ministry is messy. People have problems, and as members of the Church, it is our role to introduce those we encounter to the person of Jesus Christ as their Savior and Lord who will diminish the destructive power of worldly powers if we but cling to him. If our goal is to avoid problems altogether, then we should just close up shop, go home, and do nothing. Christ established the Church so that we could bring his grace and truth to people in an effort to overcome or reach beyond their problems and grow in grace. Groups create environments where health and growth can take place. It is a way in which we fulfill the mission of Jesus to make disciples.

4. It takes too much energy and effort to launch groups.

Yes, it will take energy and effort to launch groups, but the reduction in the demand for pastoral care alone makes the point. Small groups help members of our parish learn to care for one another. It will be much less effort in the long run investing in groups.

5. I don't need any more friends, especially strangers.

Perhaps you do have enough friends. If so, count yourself blessed. But you get into a small group not because you need friends but because you need friends in *faith*. You need friends that you gather with on a regular basis to discuss scripture and how it intersects with your life. You need some people who understand the struggles and joys that come from following Jesus and the roles and responsibilities you have in life. Small groups are not about just meeting more friends but having friends in faith and being a friend in faith for others.

6. I don't know the Bible very well. I am not holy enough.

You don't need to know the Bible at all, and small groups are not meant to be "holy huddles" for the most pious people in our parishes. The point of groups is to take you wherever you are on your faith journey and help you grow as a Christ follower through faith-based conversations and connections.

| Appendix C |

Scripture Verses on Small Groups

Throughout this book we have quoted scripture passages that support small groups and can help you as you get started. Below are some of our favorite verses you can consult when making a case for small groups in your parish.

Genesis 2:18
The LORD God said: It is not good for the man to be alone. I will make a helper suited to him.

Psalm 133:1
How good and how pleasant it is, when brothers dwell together as one!

Proverbs 13:20
Walk with the wise and you become wise,
but the companion of fools fares badly.

Proverbs 15:22
Plans fail when there is no counsel,
but they succeed when advisers are many.

Proverbs 17:17
A friend is a friend at all times,
and a brother is born for the time of adversity.

Proverbs 27:17
Iron is sharpened by iron; one person sharpens another.

Ecclesiastes 4:9–10
Two are better than one: They get a good wage for their toil.
If the one falls, the other will help the fallen one.
But woe to the solitary person!
If that one should fall, there is no other to help.

Ecclesiastes 4:12
Where one alone may be overcome, two together can resist.
A three-ply cord is not easily broken.

Matthew 18:19–20
[Jesus said,] "Again, [amen,] I say to you,
if two of you agree on earth about anything for which they are
to pray,
it shall be granted to them by my heavenly Father.
For where two or three are gathered together in my name,
there am I in the midst of them."

Mark 2:5
When Jesus saw their faith, he said to the paralytic,
"Child, your sins are forgiven."

John 13:34–35
[Jesus said,] "I give you a new commandment: love one another.
As I have loved you, so you also should love one another.
This is how all will know that you are my disciples,
if you have love for one another."

Acts 2:42
They devoted themselves to the teaching of the apostles
and to the communal life,
to the breaking of the bread and to the prayers.

Acts 2:46
Every day they devoted themselves
to meeting together in the temple area
and to breaking bread in their homes.
They ate their meals with exultation and sincerity of heart.

Acts 5:42
And all day long, both at the temple and in their homes,
they did not stop teaching and proclaiming the Messiah, Jesus.

Romans 1:11–12
For I long to see you,
that I may share with you some spiritual gift
so that you may be strengthened,
that is, that you and I may be mutually encouraged
by one another's faith, yours and mine.

Romans 12:9–10
Let love be sincere; hate what is evil, hold on to what is good;
love one another with mutual affection;
anticipate one another in showing honor.

Romans 15:7
Welcome one another, then, as Christ welcomed you,
for the glory of God.

Galatians 6:2
Bear one another's burdens,
and so you will fulfill the law of Christ.

Ephesians 4:1–3
I, then, a prisoner for the Lord, urge you
to live in a manner worthy of the call you have received,
with all humility and gentleness, with patience,
bearing with one another through love,

striving to preserve the unity of the spirit through the bond of peace.

Ephesians 4:32
Be kind to one another,
compassionate, forgiving one another
as God has forgiven you in Christ.

Colossians 3:12–13
Put on then, as God's chosen ones, holy and beloved,
heartfelt compassion, kindness, humility, gentleness, and patience,
bearing with one another and forgiving one another,
if one has a grievance against another;
as the Lord has forgiven you, so must you also do.

1 Thessalonians 2:8
With such affection for you, we were determined to share with you
not only the gospel of God, but our very selves as well,
so dearly beloved had you become to us.

1 Thessalonians 5:11
Therefore, encourage one another
and build one another up, as indeed you do.

Hebrews 3:12–13
Take care, brothers, that none of you may have
an evil and unfaithful heart, so as to forsake the living God.
Encourage yourselves daily while it is still "today,"
so that none of you may grow hardened by the deceit of sin.

Hebrews 10:25
We should not stay away from our assembly,
as is the custom of some, but encourage one another.

James 5:16
Therefore, confess your sins to one another,
and pray for one another, that you may be healed.
The fervent prayer of a righteous person is very powerful.

1 John 4:11–12
Beloved, if God so loved us, we also must love one another.
No one has ever seen God. Yet, if we love one another,
God remains in us, and his love is brought to perfection in us.

| Appendix D |

Small Group Covenant/ Agreement/Commitments

A group agreement establishes a few basic commitments that group members make to one another. The commitments may change over time and should represent all group members.

Sample Agreement

The mission of our group is to love God, love others, and make disciples through faith-based conversations, support, and accountability.

Our group will meet for 90 minutes weekly on Wednesday evenings from 7:00 to 8:30 to reflect on and discuss the current parish small-group curriculum, or other mutually agreed upon content. If a member cannot attend a group meeting, the member should text the group members prior to the meeting day.

Our group values:

Attendance: We value everyone's presence so that we can mutually learn from one another and build relationships.

Confidentiality: What happens in the group stays in the group. Gossip sabotages connection and community.

Growth-Oriented: We are always looking for ways to grow in our faith as a group. We will focus on how to follow Jesus and put his teachings into action in our lives.

Respect & Authenticity: As a group, we will respect each other's contributions to the group discussion. We will not cut others off while they are talking or talk over people. We will keep the discussion centered on what is directly affecting the group members and the curriculum. We will avoid advice-giving and "fixing" others and instead help members reason things out on their own. We will support and pray for each member.

Sharing Responsibilities: This group is not solely the leader's group, this is our group. We will participate by taking turns leading the discussion or part of the discussion, hosting the online platform, planning events for the group, following up on absent group members, and handling other responsibilities that come along.

Serving: Our group will find ways to love and serve one another both within the group and outside the group in the community. As needs arise, together the group will help to meet the need.

It is my intention to honor this covenant.

Small-group member _____ Date _____

Group leader _____Date _____

Rebuilt Resources

Church of the Nativity
20 East Ridgely Road, Timonium, MD

ChurchNativity.com.
Nativity Online: www.churchnativity.com/nativity-online/
Facebook: facebook.com/churchnativity

Rev. Michael White
X (Fr. Michael): @nativitypastor
Make Church Matter (blog): nativitypastor.tv

Rebuilt

Rebuilt Parish Association: rebuiltparish.com
Rebuilt Parish Podcast: rebuiltparish.podbean.com

Rebuilt Books

White, Michael, and Tom Corcoran. *ChurchMoney: Rebuilding the Way We Fund Our Mission*. Notre Dame, IN: Ave Maria Press, 2019.

———. *Rebuilding Your Message: Practical Tools to Strengthen Your Preaching and Teaching*. Notre Dame, IN: Ave Maria Press, 2015.

———. *Rebuilt: Awakening the Faithful, Reaching the Lost, Making Church Matter*. Notre Dame, IN: Ave Maria Press, 2013.

———. *Rebuilt Faith: A Handbook for Skeptical Catholics*. Notre Dame, IN: Ave Maria Press, 2023.

———. *The Rebuilt Field Guide: Ten Steps for Getting Started*. Notre Dame, IN: Ave Maria Press, 2016.

———. *Seriously, God? Making Sense of Life Not Making Sense*. Notre Dame, IN: Ave Maria Press, 2021.

———. *Tools for Rebuilding: 75 Really, Really Practical Ways to Make Your Parish Better*. Notre Dame, IN: Ave Maria Press, 2013.

Fr. Michael White is a priest of the Archdiocese of Baltimore, pastor of Church of the Nativity in Timonium, Maryland, and cofounder of Rebuilt Parish—an organization designed to rebuild parishes for growth and health.

White is the coauthor of the bestselling book *Rebuilt*—which narrates the story of Nativity's rebirth—*Tools for Rebuilding, Rebuilding Your Message, The Rebuilt Field Guide*, and *ChurchMoney*. He is also coauthor of *Seriously, God?* and the bestselling Messages series for Advent and Lent.

During White's tenure as pastor at Church of the Nativity, the church has almost tripled in weekend attendance. More importantly, commitment to the mission of the Church has grown, demonstrated by the significant increase of giving, service in ministry, and much evidence of genuine spiritual renewal.

White earned his bachelor's degree from Loyola University Maryland and his graduate degrees in sacred theology and ecclesiology from the Pontifical Gregorian University in Rome.

In 2023, White and Corcoran were honored by Pope Francis with the Pro Ecclesia et Pontifice Award for outstanding service to Church and Pope.

Tom Corcoran has served Church of the Nativity in Timonium, Maryland, in a variety of roles that give him a unique perspective on parish ministry and leadership. First hired as a youth minister, Corcoran has also served as coordinator of children's ministry and director of small groups. He is lay associate to the pastor and is responsible for weekend message development, strategic planning, and staff development. Corcoran also is the president of Rebuilt Parish—an organization designed to rebuild parishes for growth and health.

Corcoran is the coauthor of the bestselling book *Rebuilt*—which narrates the story of Nativity's rebirth—*Tools for Rebuilding, Rebuilding Your Message, The Rebuilt Field Guide*, and *ChurchMoney*. He is also coauthor of *Seriously, God?* and the bestselling Messages series for Advent and Lent.

In 2023, White and Corcoran were honored by Pope Francis with the Pro Ecclesia et Pontifice Award for outstanding service to Church and Pope.

churchnativity.com
rebuiltparish.com
http://rebuiltparish.com/podcast
Facebook: churchnativity
X: @churchnativity
Instagram: @churchnativity
Facebook: rebuilt parish
Instagram: @rebuiltparish
YouTube: @rebuiltparish

Bishop Adam J. Parker is auxiliary bishop and vicar general of the Archdiocese of Baltimore.

rebuilt
PARISH

**Making Disciples by Helping
Parishes Make Disciples**

Rebuilt Parish is a Catholic parish renewal
movement that is boldly impacting pastors and parish
staff, providing them with the process and tools
they need to refocus on reaching the un-churched,
creating a clear discipleship path to grow their parish
and revitalizing their parish culture.

Scan here for additional resources that
will support you in building and growing
small groups in your parish or visit
rebuiltparish.com/transformativesmallgroups.

www.rebuiltparish.com

MORE BOOKS IN
THE REBUILT PARISH SERIES

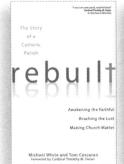 

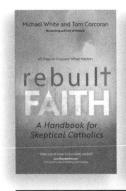 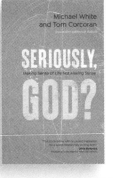

PERFECT
FOR SMALL-GROUP
BOOK STUDIES!

Both small-group
books come with **FREE**
resources and videos
to help lead your groups.